Tootsie Never Missed a Beat!
(Clarence Adolphus Bean)

Written by Cee Bennett-Rogers
Based on narrations from Clarence Adolphus Bean

ISBN-13: **978-0-947481-71-1**

Dedication

I dedicate this book to all my family members, and existing fellow musicians that I have had the pleasure to perform with over the years.

Acknowledgements

My thanks and appreciation to:
Cee Bennett-Rogers - the researcher and writer of this book; my daughter Donna Raynor, who took the initial steps to instigate its completion; and Grandson, Domico Watson, for the professional creation of the book cover.

Thanks also to Dale Butler and Winston Rogers for their photographic contributions; and again to Winston Rogers, for the additional information he imparted to support the writing of this book.

Book cover design and graphics: Domico Watson
Book cover write-up: Cee Bennett-Rogers
Photo images: Tootsie Bean's collection, Winston Rogers, Dale Butler
(Music on the Rock publication), and Royal Gazette (1).

Additional sources of information:
The Bean family archive, Music on the Rock publication, and The Royal Gazette .

Contents

Foreword (Cee Bennett-Rogers)

Clarence Adolphus Bean, otherwise known, as Tootsie Bean, or Clarence Tootsie Bean, is a talented, renowned, Bermudian musician and a living legend, both locally and abroad. As an accomplished drummer, Mr Bean is equally highly respected by fellow musicians, in Bermuda and the USA, for his exceptional skills. His career, spanned a period of seventy-five years, during which, he tutored and inspired many budding musicians to perfect and utilise their talent, some of whom have since coined a name for themselves in the world of drumming.

A few factors (including the Bermuda Gombeys), sparked Mr Bean's interest in drumming, and led to the awareness of his talent. In the earlier years of his youth, his talent surfaced naturally, growing in intensity through lessons, regular practice, and encouragement from family and experienced musicians. I suspect that the very first time Clarence Tootsie Bean picked up a drumstick; (or something resembling a drumstick), he knew exactly what to do with it; and undoubtedly, in years to come, rapidly absorbed the knowledge and skills taught, to set him on the path to achieving his goal.

On our first encounter, Mr Bean's smile and gentle, modest approach, (befitting for the gentleman that he is), hid the fullness of his achievements, and the extent to which he was, and is still valued in the music world. I soon came to realise that his brilliant smile, portrayed throughout his performing years, was an expression of the great love he had for music; and the satisfaction felt, when in his element performing on stage.

Mr Bean's ego is notably very contained, given that he is a highly skilled and experienced drummer/percussionist, featured on several recordings. He had shared his talent throughout tours and performances with different bands in many parts of the world, which in effect expanded his horizons. Added to Mr Bean's repertoire, are the unimaginable performances at the 1993 US Presidential Inauguration, the Lincoln Centre, Carnegie Hall, and Ronnie Scots Jazz Club. He considered himself privileged (although he was extremely worthy), to have performed with great musicians such as, Lance Hayward, Ernest Leader, Winslow Fox, Etta Jones, Ruth Brown and Irene Reid. These were times in his career that he especially treasured; along with the time spent performing with Bobby Forrester and as a valued member of "The Countsmen" band.

Reporter Nancy Acton, regarded Mr Bean as a man "blessed with effortless charm and a smile that could melt chocolate", and I for one second that personal view. One statement that I felt sure, Mr Bean's peers would applaud, is Nancy's description of his talent. In her calculation, Mr Bean "may not be the tallest of men, but in terms of talent, his stature is king-sized."

Mr Bean recently celebrated his eighty-ninth birthday, and as a survivor of his musical acquaintances, he feels blessed to be around to enjoy life with his family. It is quite possible that some of his acquaintances, might not have known what he was doing in the years spent away from home and family, but now here it is, outlined in print for all to read.

Although retired from performing, Mr Bean has shown continued interests in music, and based on his personal assessment, has eloquently expressed his opinion of modern compilations. Furthermore, one could also infer that his previous commitment to playing the drums at church, strongly indicates that despite his age, drumming, will forever be in his heart.

Chapter 1: The Earlier Days

My life to date has been very fulfilling, as I am sure most of my associates and family members would agree, mainly because the response to the display of my talent at home and abroad has exceeded my expectations. The timing of the completion of this book would place me in my eighty-ninth year, and I sometimes question, *'Where did all the years go?'* As it stands, I cannot believe I have survived to this stage of my life, and considered as one of the last of Bermuda's Jazz legends.

When I think of the different situations experienced over the years, I have to thank the Lord for bringing me this far. Had it not been for him, I don't know if I would have survived to be here today to narrate my tale. I sincerely hope that the writing of this book will serve as an inspiration to other musicians and young people; in particular those youths (male or female), who possess the potential to become talented musicians, along with the interest and determination to pursue their musical goals.

Most people living in the beautiful island of Bermuda in the Atlantic Ocean, will know or have some knowledge of the location of Government Gate in Pembroke Parish. This is where I was born on the 14th August 1930 to parents, Alton Bean and Alice Bean (nee Joell). Apparently, when I was born, my sister Erminie, thought I looked like a Tootsie Roll, and looking at my photos taken back then, I cannot imagine why! For those of you who do not know, or can't recall what a Tootsie Roll is, it's just a candy with a chocolaty texture - a creation of Austrian, Leo Hirshfield. Leo had named this candy after his daughter, whose nickname, incidentally was "Tootsie".

For as long as I can remember, I was known by the nickname Tootsie. Most Bermudians in my days had a nickname …it was just part of the culture! I recall having a teacher by the name of Tootsie Richardson, and this was my first encounter with a person whose proper name was actually the same as my nickname. Erminie gave me the name "Tootsie", because of my so-called, Tootsie Roll looks, and growing up, it didn't help that I just happened to love chocolate, and chicken too, but I will tell you more about my chicken craze later.

Officially, my proper title is Clarence Adolphus Bean, but predominantly throughout my music career, people referred to me with that added "Tootsie" title - Tootsie Bean, Tootsie Clarence Bean, or Clarence Tootsie Bean. I was happy to be addressed by any

1

of these titles, as long as I had continued recognition as a talented drummer.

I am the youngest of my siblings – the *surprise child* as it were! My mother had reached a point in her life, where she thought *"age"* would restrict her from having more descendants and then surprisingly, I came along! Considering all my siblings and their offspring, you could say that I came from a very large family. My parents, Alice and Alton Bean, had seven children in total: Winifred (also known as Pancie), Vivian, Erminie, Phyllis, Jamie and my eldest brother Arthur, who the family nicknamed "Bingo" due to his love for this gambling game, and me as the last addition.

As my siblings were considerably older, it is fair to say that there were times when I felt like I was growing up practically by myself. I am not one for broadcasting sob stories about my life, or that of my family, but admittedly, with the exception of my sister Ermine, there was hardly any interaction between my siblings and me. I was inclined to think this was due to our age gap and differences in interests, and therefore declined to fuss about it. Now, time has flown by, and whilst saddened over the years by the passing of all my siblings, I feel fortunate and blessed to be the only surviving child for my parents.

My mother and I had a loving, amicable relationship throughout my childhood. I knew she always worked, but if you were to ask what she did and where, I couldn't say exactly, because as a child; preoccupied with my own thoughts, I had very little concern about such things. As for my father, from what I understood, he was a Stonecutter by trade. We had a relatively good relationship; but I still have some difficulty, recalling anything more substantial about his life. The fact that my parents separated when I was twelve years old, probably accounted for my lack of knowledge. My mother however, never remarried; instead, she chose to remain devoted to her motherly duties. She was a good parent - always there for support if necessary, and as a young man growing up, facing life as it was then, that was all I expected from her.

After my parent's separation, my mother and I resided with my second, eldest sister Winifred, in North Street, Hamilton. For reasons unknown, Winifred and I could not exist amicably in the same space, so to avoid aggravation, my mother thought it best for me to reside with my sister Ermine (Alice Erminie Simmons). At the time, she was living in Tills Hill, near Courts Street in Pembroke Parish; and moving in with her, was just what I needed to see me through my adolescent years. Erminie provided essential stability during my youth and beyond, and had never failed to look after my well-being during those growing, influential years. With the help of her husband Maxwell Simmons, she facilitated the start of my music career, and was a great source of encouragement as my career progressed.

Erminie used to tease me relentlessly about my love for chicken, because back in the day, this was my favourite source of protein. I could eat this morning, noon and night, fried, baked, stewed, or whatever – as long as it tasted good! When I sniffed that lovely aroma, I couldn't help myself! I would sneak into Erminie's kitchen, and regardless of the size, would pick, and pick at that tasty chicken, until the succulent flesh was reduced to a fraction of its size. Her annoyance must have filtered through every time she saw the remains of her chicken … in fact, I am sure that it did! I can hear her now, yelling as she did back then, *Tootsie…what happen to my chicken!*' and usually, this was my cue to disappear quickly from the house.

Ermine never attempted to punish me for my sneaky, chicken feasting, which in the end became merely a joke between us. Years later, whenever we visited or ran into each other somewhere, she would always tease me with this question that, I presumed she expected me to answer each time, 'Tootsie … do you still like chicken?'

Image of a Tootsie Roll

Chapter 2: How It All Began

To begin my tale, firstly I have to say that life in the 1930s and some decades after were relatively harder than it is now in twenty-first century Bermuda. Things were not that easy for musicians seeking recognition - they had to work hard! Most of those musicians fortunate enough to get the exposure and the fame they so desired, started out with some indication of their aspirations. They could identify their talents or musical interest from a young age, however small, or great at the time, and focused on doing the things that would perfect their skills. In fact, I can proudly say that I was one of those musicians. From my youth, drumming was a permanent fixture in my thoughts. I could feel it in my blood and in my veins and was just rearing to go!

My drumming interest emerged during my time at Central School, or quite possibly before then. I began my primary education there at about six or seven years old, and from what I recall, in those days, music programs were not included in the school curriculum. From such an early age, I was constantly banging sticks on anything within my reach, trying to imitate the sound of a drum. I must have driven my parents, crazy with the noise. Their frequent yelling, 'Clarence … stop making that noise!' echoed in my ears, but I don't think I took much notice. I was too busy tuning into the drum sounds in my head, just waiting to manifest.

The traditional Bermudian Gombeys, with origins steeped in the Island's history extending back to slavery days, was a real fascination for me at the time. I was frequently experimenting with Gombey drum sounds from the age of seven, and after a while, took steps to organise a Gombey group with my friends. We designed and made our costumes, using crocus bag material (the ones used to package potatoes), and went in search of large tin cans to make the drums. I remembered it took extreme effort, to repeatedly, pound these tin cans into shape, to obtain a sound similar, to the real Gombey drums, and when we sampled them, I was so pleased that it worked!

Dressed in our crocus bag costumes, with tin-can drums strung around our necks, we toured the neighbourhood, doing our best to imitate the real Gombeys. We had followers in the community, who swayed or danced to the sound of our drums, but what was missing was the "treat". Unlike the other mature Gombey groups, we rarely received the tips we deserved for our efforts that was part of the tradition, and at times we were so disappointed.

Imitating the Gombey drum sounds in those developmental years was great fun; and a rich experience that aided my familiarity with varied drum rhythms. It wasn't long before I began to realise that creating drum sounds, came naturally to me. With this awareness came a strong urge to play tunes on a whole drum kit, with snare, bass drum, cymbals etc. It also highlighted my growing passion for the drums, along with the belief that I had a God-given talent; and were on the verge of exploring my potential, starting with the help, I would receive from my guardians.

My brother-in-law Maxwell was very musical and an excellent tap dancer. Whilst he danced, he would skilfully play the "Bones" between his fingers that created a rhythmic sound similar, to the Spanish Castanet. His additional jobs as a club bouncer and gardener for Bermuda Parks, gathering flowers for the Outerbridge family, and for Erminie to peddle, brought in an extra income. Maxwell treated me very well. He was the first to notice my serious obsession and natural drumming talent, expressed as mentioned before, through tapping drum sounds on everything within my reach, and doing odd things, like shining my shoes to a rhythm. I remember Maxwell asking me once to shine his shoes, and when I stated that, 'I am gonna play you a tune as am shining them!' his quirky expression left me smiling, but I knew he understood exactly what I was about to do.

When Ermine and Maxwell purchased my first drum kit, (an instrument I had always dreamt of possessing), I was surprised by the lengths to which they would go to help fulfil my dreams. This beautiful drum kit was so heavy, it weighed more than I did, and seated around it, I could just about see over the top. I have memories of sitting on the porch of Erminie's house, practicing my drumming; and even in those early days, I never failed to attract an audience from the neighbourhood, (including my friends) that would gather to watch and hear me play.

At the age of eleven, during World War II in 1941, Maxwell arranged for me to have lessons, with the talented drummer and saxophonist, Ernest (Ernie) Leader. Ernest was tutored by Willie Smith, and Mark Williams, and he became one of the most prominent, musicians of that era. He had started out very similar to me at an early age, experimenting with drum sounds, so you could say we had an understanding right from the word go! Whereas I had practiced on tin cans or, anything I could find he did this on a trunk with his heels. Later, American musicians influenced his style of drumming, which was another similarity we both, shared.

Ernest Leader's patience as a tutor did not go unnoticed. His two-year tutelage served to improve my skills during those difficult War years that affected Bermuda. I suppose being a young boy overall, the War didn't bother me much. I can recall the military presence on the Island, the blackouts, the covered lampposts that never shone at night, and of course the dreaded rations! Those years were bleak, but for some unknown reason, I never felt scared! My motivation was spiralling, so I focused my attention on Ernest's lessons instead of the War. As a tutee, I worked very hard to polish my skills and was naturally a fast learner. Ernest's approach to tutoring, increased the passion and motivation within me to grasp whatever he taught me, including how to accompany him on the drums, whilst he played the piano. My ambition to succeed, was firmly in my mind then, and this was a step in that direction.

In hindsight, there is a lot that I could say about the benefits of having a good, patient tutor like Ernest. I may not have fully realised it then, but Ernest's tutelage was the start of learning how to accompany a performer as a drummer - a skill that I would come to value greatly, in future years.

Traditional Bermudian Gombeys performing on the grounds of a house on the Island. (Photo by Winston O. Rogers)

Chapter 3: Debut Performance

The Ernest Leader Orchestra was a popular band during the War, despite the closure of some hotels and the decline of the tourist trade. These issues amounted to reduced employment for some musicians, which was evidently not a major problem for this

band. Ernest assembled his orchestra after performing with Lance Hayward and Winslow Fox, and had frequently played at the US Bases and major operating hotels, including the Inverurie.

His Orchestra was also a popular feature at the Coral Island Club and The Band Room venue on Band Room Lane, famous for its regular dances, and traditional, Coconut Shy games. Black folks in those days certainly had a "ball" at the Band Room, despite the entrance fees that depending on the type of function, ranged from one to ten shillings. Noticeably, some people had no objections to paying the higher cost, especially if they were particularly seeking to have a good time and felt certain of obtaining this.

In 1943 at the age of thirteen, Ernest decided my talent and skills were at the right level for a debut performance at the famous Band Room. At such a young age, the anticipation of doing my first live performance to a paid audience was at the very least, daunting. After all, this performance would be different, from having my friends as an audience, listening to my free, practiced sessions on Ermine's porch; and just thinking about it was enough to escalate my anxiety. As to be expected, thoughts of pulling out of the performance clouded my mind, before I felt swayed by the persistence of Ernest's band musicians. They certainly had more confidence in my ability to perform to an audience, than I did at the time.

On the night of my debut, I could feel the hum of the audience all around me, as I walked onto the bandstand, looking sharp, and nervously took my seat behind my drum kit. Attempting to peek over the top, as expected, the audience could just about see my head, which did nothing to ease my fears. Despite my anxiety, the aim was to perform to a standard that would meet the band's expectations; because even with my limited experience, I knew the importance of setting the mood for dancing. This was what the, audience wanted, and had paid their money to do.

As I proceeded with my performance somehow, I managed to calm my nerves to an extent, to accompany the band, and play the drums to ease into the rhythm of the swing, which was the trend at the time. As the clock kept ticking, I felt my fears fading and my confidence lifting, and just as I was beginning to feel more relaxed, there was an unexpected interruption. This unnerved me for a moment before I recognised the voice as that of my best friend, Winston Gumbs. I could hear him yelling more than once, 'I can't hear you …I can't hear you down the back!'

It wasn't clear to me, why Winston could not hear the drums from where he sat. Perhaps I was playing the drums softer than usual, due to my initial bout of nerves, but regardless of the reason, this was an untimely, unwelcome distraction that was difficult to ignore, and would very likely affect my concentration and focus. The thought had also crossed my mind that he was winding me up, so I decided to call his bluff. 'Why don't you come up here and play the drums!' I yelled towards the back.

Winston rose from his seat and surprisingly walked boldly up to the stage, without any interference from the band members, who probably viewed the scenario enfolding before them, as additional entertainment for the audience. I watched silently as he sat behind my kit, picked up the drumsticks and attempted to play the drums, but it just, wasn't flowing! Evidently, he lacked the skills to handle the drumsticks correctly, and to be honest I had anticipated this. Playing the drums using my raw talent and rapidly emerging skills, made me feel totally at home. To my friend, this appeared to be an easy task, but it was not! It required certain skills and coordination, mastered only with regular practice, and a natural aptitude that, without meaning to brag, I have always possessed.

After Winston solemnly left the stage, I resumed my place behind the drum kit and continued playing with the band until the show ended. Eagerly seeking acknowledgement, I scanned the room for my tutor, whose facial expression said it all. I had no way of knowing how Ernest felt about Winston's disruption. What I knew for sure was that both he and his encouraging band members were pleased with my performance. This coupled with the response from the audience, was enough to make my head swirl, and I felt sure that I would experience more of this elation in the years to come.

Chapter 4: Juggling My Time

Following my debut performance, I became a member of Ernest's band and with some difficulty, juggled my time between my life as a student and a musician, frequently performing at the US military bases. In the initial stages of my primary education at Central School (now known as Victor Scott School), my reputation was quite good. I was progressing well with my studies, and rarely in trouble with my teacher, Tootsie Richardson, but that was before I entered the ninth grade with my cousins, Sonny Wilson and Sherman Hollis. For some reason, I was frequently getting into trouble and losing concentration at times, which affected my grades, and the fact that I was juggling my education with performances at the American bases, didn't do much to improve the situation. Things were just as I had stated in a 2012 interview with the Royal Gazette; "Going to school during the days and working nights, was quite an experience for a young man like me!"

There were two US Bases in Bermuda, located in Somerset and St Georges, and these housed a large percentage of military personnel, seeking to be entertained. There were limited numbers of foreign musicians on the Island due to the War, and although work was relatively scarce, this gave some local musicians the opportunity to perform at the US bases, as well as the operating hotels that were keen to entertain the military. The military personnel always arranged transportation from my home, to whatever base I was performing at, and as far as my friends were concerned, this was an awesome arrangement. When the military bus pulled up to collect me, in the excitement, they never failed to shout out, loud and clear, 'Tootsie … here comes your bus!'

Hearing this, off I would go, regardless of whatever we were doing at the time. My friends usually seized the opportunity to toss my drum kit onto the military bus, and I followed quickly thereafter…they would throw me in right behind the kit! Luckily, neither my kit nor I sustained any damages or injuries, but maybe I just cannot recall that happening!

I was not the only one travelling on these military buses back then. The bus drivers had instructions to collect female passengers from Hamilton and transport them to the US Bases to entertain the soldiers. Whilst us band members were having a good time performing, these women were having fun dancing with the soldiers, and at the end, the driver would transport us all, back to our pick-up points.

I was gaining experience and significant knowledge of band performance, along with an improved confidence, and becoming increasingly aware of the plus and minus side of this type of life. I am referring here, to the fact that my performances with the band, not only affected my education, it was reducing the precious playtime I usually had with my friends. This peer group interaction was fun, and indeed necessary to fulfil the intricate part of growing up at this stage of my life. It allowed for quality time with my peers that I greatly missed, when the military whisked me off to perform. The problem was, after the gigs, even with the convenient, military transportation arrangements, it was impossible to return home before dusk. By the time they dropped me off, my playmates had all returned home, and at these times; despite the performance buzz, my life felt a bit empty.

Erminie and I had moved from Tills Hill to her husband's house opposite the Devonshire Recreation Ground, where I resided for some time, but most of my friends, were still residing in Government Gate where I was born. Visiting my friends after a performance was both difficult and risky, and I will explain why. Back then, Government Gate was an area in Bermuda with certain, "known rules", if you get my meaning! My friends and I knew that if you did not reside there, unless you were looking for trouble; you were definitely not supposed to be seen there!

Despite the playtime issue, working with Ernest Leader enabled my professional progression. Being the youngest in this band, the older, experienced musicians, advised me at every opportunity, and regardless of the topic, I always showed my appreciation for their assistance. As quoted in the publication, *"Music on the Rock",* Ernest was known to give, "every young player a chance to play music without qualifications, as long as they had the desire to play". I was one of those young players, lucky enough to have had the chance to prove my worth and commitment as a performer; and one of those, who benefited greatly from the opportunity Ernest Leader willing gave to kick-start my career.

Chapter 5: Stepping Out with The Bands

It got to the point where the yearning to free myself from the constraints of a double life was increasing. Trying to cope with this strained lifestyle was difficult and as stated to my sister Erminie, leaving school to find employment was high on my agenda. Despite my yearning, it was not until after my brother-in-law, Maxwell Simmons died, that I finally hung up my slate, and moved on to the next stage of my life. Unfortunately, Maxwell had died relatively young, so Erminie had the sole responsibility of supporting their two sons, Mickey and Ardie Simmons, and of course, since my mother was still residing with my older sister Winifred, she had the continued task of being my guardian.

Leaving school, freed up my time to train as a carpenter with Sam Thomas, which proved its usefulness in terms of earning extra funds. With my school years behind me, Erminie continuously encouraged my work with different bands, and therefore acting on her advice at that time was beneficial, in terms of building up my expertise to perform in different venues. Some of these venues were highly regarded hotels such as, The Bermudiana, Elbow Beach, Hamilton, and Southampton Princess. Other popular venues on my list included Harmony Hall, The Colonial Opera House, Unity Terrace, Shed Number One, Chilli Simons Patio, and Ocean View Pavilion that some people might remember. There was not a venue on the island I could think of in that era, where I did not have the opportunity to perform with a band.

Before TVs with multiple channels became a permanent fixture in our homes to bombard our minds, dances and band music performances were the main forms of entertainment. This was an important part of our community, so with nightclubs and dance halls operating across the Island, the nightlife as some people will recall, was very lively. New bands appeared with great musicians such as Ernest Leader, and people became familiar with seeing band members looking sharp, dressed in tuxedos, or white jackets and black trousers. The good thing about the abundance of nightclubs and dance halls was that for a while, it increased the availability of work, and gave musicians such as myself, the opportunity to be in demand across the Island. I felt at first that these exciting days would go on forever, but as the years rolled on, things as I knew it began to change with the times.

It was a well-known fact that many musicians during my time had to secure day jobs to supplement their main income, which in some cases could hardly meet their financial needs. Ernest Leader, for example, did two jobs to increase his income and sometimes I did more. With my carpentry skills, I found work as a carpenter, and made some of the lovely furniture in my home. At one point, I drove a van for a local bakery and a truck for the Public Works Department, which both required possession of a valid, driving licence. I didn't mess around in those days! As soon as I was old enough to get a licence - I made sure to do what was needed to obtain one.

I was asked how I managed to cope with doing day jobs in addition to the nightly gigs. Well … I was young and in my prime in those days, with the energy and motivation to work hard to support myself. Lance Hayward was firmly against musicians doing day jobs after nightly performances, because he felt strongly that this would affect their practice time, and development. Perhaps this was true to an extent, but with my strong focus on pursuing a music career and perfecting my skills, doing a day job aided, rather than deterred my development.

The opportunity to do more gigs with Ernest Leader's band, increased my income, and effectively raised my performance standards. Similarly, I was very grateful to those foreign musicians, sailing into St Georges and Front Street ports on cruise ships, whose valuable tips enhanced my performance and had some input in my progress. Having benefitted from this type of support in my youth is partly the reason, why I took time in future years, to assist younger musicians who were eager to learn, and at those times, my patience had no boundaries.

After working with Ernest Leader for some years, I decided to join the Freddie Matthews band, to obtain more experience and a change of scene. Freddie was a talented saxophonist and clarinet player, as well as a skilled carpenter like me. His inspiration came from bandleader, Mark Williams, and his cousin, who tutored him in the art of sax playing. Freddie gained experience performing with several bands, before organising his own with skilled musicians, who could play a wide selection of music, to please the audience. When Freddie secured a contract with the American Military Base in St Georges, he divided his eight-piece band to meet the demands of the venues requesting his service, and this is where I came in!

The New Windsor Hotel in Hamilton and the popular Alexandrina Hall on Court Street that many Bermudians frequented, were just some examples of the venues, I had performed at with the Freddie Matthews' band. One of the reasons why I especially enjoyed our gigs at Alexandrina Hall was the fact that the party ravers, who would flock to see us perform, were always out to have a good time and would openly express their enjoyment for our shows.

As band members, sometimes the thought of encountering problems at a venue during one of our gigs, were the furthest thing from our minds, but such things although unanticipated, were inevitable, and Alexandrina Hall was one such place where the unexpected occurred. One year during our performance on Guy Fawkes night, there was a startling incident that immediately put a stop to our show. This happened, when a group of mischievous young people began to hurl fireworks through the venue windows, and at parked cars. The whole place erupted into chaos as the scared and panic-stricken audience, attempted to flee the building, all at the same time. Some took to screaming from the shock, whilst others forced their way through the entrance.

Our show was evidently ruined, and as it did not appear that the venue would return to any form of normality anytime soon, we decided to do the only thing possible. We packed up our band instruments at high speed and exited the building along with the crowd. To my knowledge, the Government ban on firework displays without a permit, came into existence, partly because of this untimely, inappropriate incident.

Apart from Alexandrina Hall, I performed regularly at the military bases and the lovely Castle Harbour Hotel (now the Tuckers Point Hotel), as the youngest member of Freddie's Band; taking tips from the older musicians. We shared the bandstand with the Earl Darrell Quartet, and made sure to observe the strict hotel rules we encountered there. In those days, musicians had to literally pack up their instruments and leave the premises after a performance, or risk the embarrassment of being asked to leave. Nowadays it is very different for musicians. After a performance, they can relax in the bar and enjoy the facilities, but we were denied such privileges back then.

The relationship and rapport developed with Freddie Matthews and his musicians remained solid throughout the six years performing with the band; and as expected, I matured in terms of my confidence and skills. When the time came to move on, I do not believe Freddie wanted me to leave, but the decision was partly due to my desire to gain more experience to further my career.

For a short time, I toured the hotels and venues with the talented pianist and poet Alvin Brangman. He was a well loved and highly rated, musician in Bermuda and was inducted in the Music Hall of Fame at Shine Hayward's Music Studio. The last time I performed with Alvin, was at a hotel in Point Shears, in Fairyland, Pembroke Parish. This was another area, similar to Tuckers Point, where the wealthy resided, and they were the type of folks that enjoyed and supported Alvin's great band performances that I was a part of. The experience gained from performing briefly with this highly skilled musician and his band members, came in handy over the years. Funnily enough, Alvin thought I was deserving of the nickname "Rascal", due to my mischievous looking eyes, that were clearly invisible to me in my mirror. Nevertheless, he was an artist that I had admired, respected, and enjoyed performing with and evidently, he viewed me in the same manner. To me, he will always be one of the Island's great musicians that will never be forgotten.

Legendary trumpet and trombone player, Ghandi Burgess, and I were both trained and skilled in the use of our preferred instruments. As friends, we have always treated each other with respect, not only for our repertoire, but also for who we were as individuals. After studying at the New York School of Music, Ghandi started out quite young in the music industry, building up a repertoire that included performances with greats such as Nina Simone, Ben E. King, The Temptations and more. At some point, he held the musical director position at the Forty Thieves Night Club and Southampton Princess Hotel, where he resided as an honoured guest for about twelve years. The names of his band members are hard to recall, but I do remember that drummer, Alan Genley had tried to join the band, before Ghandi offered the position to my son Shelton.

Ghandi Burgess was noted as a master musician and musical genius of a high calibre, who was on par with the world's best musicians. Throughout our time working together, I honestly felt that Ghandi's skills were way ahead of his time, and perhaps ahead of even me. Under his band leadership, we performed consistently at a level that would wow the audience and highlight our professionalism and talent. Likewise, when we did gigs at the American Naval and Marine Bases, the service men always came back for more. The only problem was that these service men could not exist amicably in the same space for long. Putting it simply, the Marine soldiers did not appear to like the Navy sailors, and the Navy sailors did not appear to like the Marines. Each of these military groups, thought they were better than their counterparts that should really be respected as an equal, so you can imagine the rowdiness that occurred at times. Sometimes this was tolerable and at other times, it was downright outrageous, especially when their resentment towards each other, escalated into a brawl.

One night, we had no choice but to call it quits when a fight broke out between them during our performance. Other than the resentment on both sides that penetrated the atmosphere, no one knew what sparked the fight, and we were horrified when the violence erupted! There was so much head-banging going on, I thought all hell had broken lose! The sailors used their batons to attack the Marines (that I am sure cracked a few skulls!), and the Marines, fighting with just their bare fists, almost pounded them to the ground. They were literally smashing up the place with no concern for each other, and the devastation they would cause to the premises.

At the time, no member of Ghandi's band, including me, felt brave enough to try to stop them …we would have most likely, been crushed to death! I cannot recall if security guards were present, but then again, we were performing to the military - so who would have thought we needed security! Eventually, the manager had to call the police to break up the brawl, and he probably knew they would take their time getting there. Musicians tend not to take any chances, or try to intervene when fights like this broke out in venues. Instead, they would grab their instruments, and head for the exit, giving in to the need to protect themselves and their prized possessions. On that occasion, that is just what we did, and given the situation, no one in their right mind could blame us!

Ghandi was quite a cheerful, good-natured person - always telling jokes and doing things that created a nice atmosphere amongst the band members. One Christmas we were at a venue, looking sharp in our spotless white jackets and black pants, waiting to perform. There were plenty of food available before the show, and we ate as much as we could. The problem was, Ghandi wanted to take some of the turkey home, but having no container, he picked up a piece of turkey and shoved it in his pocket …his white, jacket pocket mind you!

The show started, and as we flowed into our performance to the delight of the audience, no one had any more thoughts about the turkey in Ghandi's pocket. We were nearly half way through the show, when to our horror we noticed the turkey sauce visibly making an appearance, through Ghandi's white jacket pocket. I expect he must have felt the same as us when he noticed it, because it was an expensive, white jacket, now stained beyond repair. What made things worse, was the fact that we all knew we were supposed to look well turned out throughout the performance … not with turkey sauce stains in our jacket pockets, attempting to say "hello" to the audience.

Perhaps the audience did or, did not notice, but from what we could see, Ghandi showed no signs of distress - his cool demeanour gave nothing away! We, on the other hand, had to keep a straight face until after the show, when we could no longer hide our amusement. To top it all, Ghandi's matter-of -fact response was a bit surprising. He glanced at us and quite leisurely said, 'Well …my jacket is soiled and will have to be replaced, but what the heck … I will still have my turkey!'

The Al Davis Orchestra was very popular on the Island, with performances at the Opera House and at the Mid Ocean Club in Tuckers Town, where they had wealthy Americans/Bermudians for an audience. Al Davis was an accomplished bandleader, whose skills some musicians believed were influenced by Ernest Leader, and at one point during the 1950s, his band was the only Bermudian band with the privilege to perform in the major hotels.

My first and only performance with Al Davis' band was at the Top Hat venue in Southampton, as an unexpected replacement for his drummer. I knew about Al Davis' reputation before my arrival, Al Davis on the other hand, had never heard of me, and neither was he aware, that I was there as his replacement drummer. My ego as always was well contained, so I had no problem with his lack of recognition. I reminded myself then that I had experienced similar situations before, and if I understood much about sit-in performances with bands, this was likely to occur again.

My intention was to do a professional sit-in performance with Al Davis' band, and as far as that went, it was more enjoyable than anticipated. Al's strict business-like leadership approach on the bandstand was admirable, and it went well with my preference for working in an organised, professionally manner. What was very pleasing in the end was Al Davis' show of appreciation for my skills, and I seriously doubted that he would fail to recognise me again after that performance.

Pianist Al Harris initially had a large band that he reduced significantly over the years, to a four-piece band. His skilled and fully trained musicians had the flexibility to play a variety of dance music, such as the waltz, jitter bug, fox trot etc. that for reasons unclear to me, Lance Hayward labelled as the *"Business Man Bounce"*. I had joined Al Harris' other band (a calypso band), for a short while, as a replacement for his previous drummer, Maxwell Lightbourne. During that time, I performed with guitarist Calvin (Cal) Hansey, upright bass guitarist Chalky Virgil and saxophonist Rags Richardson at the popular Harmony Hall Hotel. This was probably my first time playing the drums to calypso music, as opposed to jazz, but my flexibility and knack for grasping new styles and techniques aided the transition.

Apart from performing with the likes of the musicians already mentioned, back then, I was frequently moving around, alternating between bands, in a similar fashion to other musicians, who did this as a matter of survival. Working with bands that had the flexibility to play a variety of music, increased the opportunity to perform in operating venues and major hotels, as long as I was prepared to adjust to whatever style of music they chose to perform, and for me this wasn't a problem. Admittedly, during this period I felt grateful to be amongst those musicians who were in demand, either for a lengthy or brief duration.

The swing dance era that evolved from jazz, began in 1935 and maintained popularity up to and beyond my teenage years. Many people enjoyed dancing to swing, calypso, or rock and roll music that became popular in Bermuda, but those musicians playing the swing, jitterbug and the waltz were often in more demand. Some hotels had in-house nightclubs to entertain their guests, and it had reached a point, where they, along with other well-established venues, were hiring fewer jazz bands or, none at all!

The Windsor Hotel was one of the venues hiring local, jazz musicians at the time. This was the type of place that foreign, jazz lovers with an aversion to swing and other dance music, would seek to "blow off steam", as I had phrased it then. Bermuda was very segregated at the time, and so at this hotel and others, black musicians were denied the right to enter the premises via the front door. The back door was always accessible however, if they so wish to enter. It was because of this issue with segregation that my sister Ermine felt uncomfortable, and would therefore only choose to attend gigs held in venues, were black folks socialised.

On a more positive note though, whilst the jazz, swing, calypso and rock and roll years lasted, this was to some extent an exciting time for skilled, Bermudian musicians like me, who could, one way or the other, find a way to make a living, using whatever musical skills or talent they possess.

Chapter 6: Further Training

I first visited the USA in 1950 at the age of twenty, for additional training with drummer, Bay Perry, and vibraphone training with Fred Albright. When I heard, Lionel Hampton skillfully playing the vibraphone, I was instantly fascinated with it, more so than the vibraphone, and right then, and there decided to learn to play this instrument. The training was challenging mind you, but my ability to learn anything of interest, once I had a mind to do so, saw me through the process.

Before undergoing this training, playing music by ear was a natural skill, but being aware of the demand for competence in reading music, I completed music theory lessons to increase future employability with the bands. A few people and some news reporters mistakenly thought Joseph Richards was my tutor, but this was not the case. The truth is, I studied music theory with Winslow Fox, who came highly recommended by Lance Hayward - a musician that I greatly respected. Joseph Richards had tutored Lance for ten years, along with several other musicians, and it is possible that Lance had recommended Winslow, because he knew Joseph's passion was for classical music, whilst my passion, was jazz.

The lessons took place at Winslow's home, with vocalist Alan Latimore and guitarist Eugene Virgil. Later, Winslow hired me to perform at hotels such as Elbow Beach and St Georges, with Alan, Eugene, and Luther Daniels. By that time, I believed Winslow came to view me as a competent musician rather than a student, especially as we had performed well together as drummer and pianist. There were times, after my training that I accompanied Alan Latimore on the vibraphone whilst he sang, and on other occasions, played the drums as well as the vibraphone during performances.

To add to my skills, I benefitted from taking lessons with pianist, Olivette Morris, who was a skilled and firm tutor, well known for her success in tutoring many students. The piano and xylophone were instruments that I liked and could play to an extent. What was missing however, was the absence of my heart-felt interest in playing them that no tutor, could inspire, so I always returned my focus to playing the instrument that was my first love, which as you should all know by now, is the drum!

Chapter 7: Dickie Green Tour

In the1950s, Dickie Green operated a tour company in Bermuda that grew in popularity, due to the inclusion of organised dinner and dance functions, with entertainment, from the musicians and entertainers accompanying his tours. To my mind, Dickie Green showed good business sense, for the simple fact that when he planned and organised tours, they were advertised and promoted in advance, to attract patrons, both from Bermuda, and the tour countries. This strategy ensured that Mr Green secured bookings prior to his tours, to fill all the hired venues.

In 1952, Dickie Green organised a US tour, working in collaboration with Winslow Fox, that included a few Bermudian bands, and I was one of the participants. Signing up for the tour as part of Winslow's band, along with calypso singer and limbo dancer, Marlene Minks, was an exciting adventure for us all. We flew to the USA, travelling light, because as arranged, most of the venues had a drum kit, piano and other instruments on the bandstand, ready for our performance. For the tour, Mr Green had booked various nightclubs, dance halls and the Savoy Ballroom, in Lenox Avenue, Manhattan that was reportedly closed in 1958.

I performed with Winslow's band at the Savoy Ballroom that was designed with ample space, to accommodate large numbers of people. The Savoy was also known as the "black folk's nightclub, simply because to some people, it appeared like they had taken over the place. When these folks attended the events, they brought their own food (fried chicken, mac cheese, pumpkin pie etc.), and would have a feast throughout the entertainment. We played a type of dance music mixed with a calypso rhythm that was not popular in the USA then, but the audience loved it all the same! I learnt to play the drums to this type of music, simply by listening to the Latin American bands, and it felt good putting this skill into practice.

What I enjoyed most about performing at the Savoy Ballroom was the opportunity to meet other musicians, especially those, whose music I had listened to and had admired their style, or performance. At one of our performances at the Savoy we shared the same bandstand with the great, alto sax jazz player, Charles Parker, known as Charlie Yard Bird Parker, or Charlie Bird Parker. He had aided in the development of Bebop music, (a type of fast tempo jazz) that had set the standards for the musicians he inspired. Many musicians shared our bandstand, but none could touch Charlie's outstanding performance. During the tour, I had another chance to see him do a brilliant performance at the *Bird Land Club* in New York. Charlie had as people say, "fame but no fortune", but to me, he was an innovator and one of those greats who was ahead of his time; and I was sorry that apart from us sharing a bandstand, I never had the chance to perform with him.

Guitarist Norman Astwood was visiting the States during the tour and had attended the Charlie Parker show. Strangely enough, I was supposed to see Nat King Cole (another popular and great musical legend), in concert that night, and regrettably, gave my ticket away because of Norman's Uncle. He had planned to take a brief trip to Canada and as neither of them knew the route, or were in possession of a valid licence, I volunteered to drive them there. Luckily, the Canadian weather was warm for that time of year - feeling very much like a midsummer's night.

Norman and I had our hearts set on listening to some Canadian jazz musicians, to draw a comparison between them and us Bermudians. So, while his uncle went on a visit mission, we went in search of a jazz nightclub. The club we located had a jazz band, and we were getting all excited, waiting to hear them perform. What spoilt it for us was the fact that throughout the entire performance, all the vocals were sung in a foreign language. We could not understand a word of the lyrics, nor note much difference in their performance to make a comparison. In the end, Norman and I were so disappointed, we left the club feeling that it was a complete waste of our time.

Touring a country as band musicians, under the direction of a tour operator could have created certain problems, but this was not the case with Dickie Green. His tour was a well organised event, with provisions to cater for all our needs, plus the freedom to explore the areas we visited. The most important thing we had to do as a cohesive band, was to ensure regular rehearsals to optimise our performance, then chill out, refuel, and prepare ourselves for the stage curtains to rise.

Chapter 8: The Lance Hayward Days

I joined the Lance Hayward Quartet as a professional drummer and had the opportunity to perform with Lance, along with his band members at many venues. These were upright bass player Maxwell Smith, guitarists Frankie Rabain, upright bass player Gilbert Rowland, guitarists Norman Astwood, and Milt Robinson, who later joined the band. Lance Hayward was the most talented, and sought-after pianist in Bermuda, between the 1950s and 1960s, and rated as a top, professional pianist by many musicians. In my opinion, he was the best pianist Bermuda had ever produced.

Lance began playing the piano from a young age. He studied at the Perkins Institute in Massachusetts, and was tutored by Joseph Richardson. As a classically trained and self-taught jazz pianist, Lance formed the Lance Hayward Quartet in 1957, with a focus on maintaining a distinctive sound, which earned him the reputation of having one of the best bands of its time.

Prior to joining Lance's band, my intention was to become a member of the Hubert Smith's, Coral Islanders Calypso band that was very popular in Bermuda, but in the end, I decided against this and joined the Lance Hayward's Quartet. This was not a case of disloyalty; it was more to do with the choice of music. I had played the drums to jazz, calypso, and other types of music like the samba and cha-cha for eleven years in Bermuda, which served to broaden my skills. Admittedly, I liked calypso music to some extent. However, when compared with the varied jazz rhythms, the beat is very repetitive, and I knew in my heart that I could not play the drums to calypso music on a regular basis, for a lengthy period.

Some people might question my love for jazz - what so special about it? One of the reasons why I liked jazz then, and still do now, is because I have always viewed it as America's symphony - you could say that to black Americans, jazz is a form of classical music. Playing jazz is challenging, but on the other hand, this type of music has variety and scope to improvise. Listening to jazz music, you will not hear the same beat repeatedly. When you consider that there is fast jazz, slow jazz, modern jazz etc., it is interesting to know that all of these will give you a variety of different beats, sounds, rhythm, and melodies that tells a story.

If you were to listen intently to a jazz singer, you will hear meaningful lyrics in the song that might tell you something about yourself or your life! For example, I heard a story about a woman who was listening to someone singing a jazz song. The woman commented afterwards that she felt like the vocalist was singing to her especially, because everything depicted in the lyrics was all about her life.

I accepted the position to work with Lance when his previous drummer Al Butterfield migrated to the USA. As soon as Lance and I met and began working together, we hit it off straight away, and over the years, he became like a father to me. During the years we worked together in Bermuda, we accompanied many famous musicians. I was intrigued to notice that most of the foreign pianist at the hotels we performed at, ended up seeking the great Lance Hayward, for tips or advice on how to improve their performance. Teaming up with Lance's band was an opportunity that led to several performances in popular Bermudian venues such as the Jungle Room, Harmony Hall, the Forty Thieves, Elbow Beach, and the Windsor Hotel.

◀▶

The opportunity for Lance and I to make our first trip to Jamaica to tour the country, all started with Don Gibson. Don was a promoter, who organised shows with talented performers, for local hotels like Elbow Beach, the Bermudiana, Inverurie and more. When Lance and I had thoughts of seeking new ventures to expand our horizons, Don suggested the idea of going to Jamaica to explore the possibility of securing contracts, and after giving it some thought, we packed up and went off to see what Jamaica had to offer.

Securing regular contracts was the least of our worries when we arrived in Jamaica. The main problem we encountered was finding suitable bass and guitar players, so Lance had no option but to send for his Bermudian band members to make up his jazz Quartet. Guitarist Frankie Rabain and upright bass player Gilbert Rowland were the first members of the band to arrive in the first year that we performed in Jamaica. The following year, guitarist Norman Astwood, known to be the best guitarist in Bermuda at the time, joined the band to replace Frankie Rabain, who had plans to record his own album.

Another issue we faced on arrival was acceptance. Our intention was to work with the Jamaican musicians in a manner that would avoid friction, and animosity, but initially this was quite a challenge. Some of these musicians gave us a hard time. They saw us as foreign entertainers, and quite rightly felt that we would be putting them out of work in their own country. However, when Lance and I volunteered to teach Jamaican youths with an interest in music, how to play the piano and the drums, this changed the attitudes of our rival musicians. They began to treat us with respect, which overall improved the way we interacted, and in due course, one of the benefits was gaining permission to join the Jamaican Musician Union.

The Quartet: Lance, Gilbert, Norman, and I, did many tours in Jamaica. Most of our gigs were at the Half Moon Bay Hotel in Montego Bay, where Lance had secured a contract to perform with the band. Several other venues in Montego Bay and Ocho Rios had us scheduled to perform and some of these, for example, the Chatham Hotel, were fantastic places to have a gig. The Chatham Hotel was a beautiful hotel, which from what I can recall, might have been in Ocho Rios. The manager positioned our bandstand on the hotel's connecting bridge, erected over a running stream, and we had amazing views of the exquisite crabs, swimming below whilst we performed.

As our time there increased, Lance and I grew to love Jamaica, especially because regardless of where we performed, the Islanders always enjoyed our band music. At the time, the political scene between the Jamaican Labour Party (JLP) and the People's National Party (PNP) was unstable. PNP leader Norman Manley was Prime Minster and rival, Alexander Bustamante, was head of the opposition party (JLP), but I was more interested in keeping up with the music scene. Motown, Ska and Calypso music were the type of genres mostly aired on the radio. Some of the great calypso musicians were Carlos Malcolm, and the famous Byron Lee and the Dragonaires. To me, the Dragonaires were very good, but Carlos' skills and performances were outstanding. Byron Lee however fared much better, because of his rich connections that supported the band financially during hard times.

Apart from our amazing performances that frequently received good comments, and the beautiful scenery, I really enjoyed listening to the comedy radio shows of the late, Louise Bennett and Ranny Williams. As most Jamaicans of that era would agree, these comedians were hilarious. I was always sure to have a good laugh listening to their witty jokes, and only a scheduled, band performance could stop me from tuning in to their radio show.

One of the memorable things that we did in Jamaica, were the recordings at Island Record, owned by Chris Blackwell. Most people hearing the names, Island Records and Chris Blackwell simultaneously, would associate these with the famous Bob Marley. Mr Blackwell was the person who put the talented, innovated Bob Marley and the Wailers on the map and made them famous. I personally believed that when Bob Marley and the Wailers started out, they brought something new to the music world, and that was the main reason, why no other record producer apart from Chris Blackwell, would risk working with them.

Our first recording at Island Records was Chris Blackwell's first production in Jamaica, and this took place in his studio in Kingston (the capital), some distance from Montego Bay. Barbara Delissa had the task of driving us from Montego Bay, to his studio in Kingston. She was the daughter of Mr Delissa, a wealthy man, who owned the hotel booked for our stay. Travelling from Montego Bay to Kingston through the mountains and winding roads was not an easy journey to endure, because back then, the Jamaican roads were very different in comparison to how they are now. I don't think I have ever seen roads like these, or have had such a bumpy ride since, so as you can imagine, when we finally arrived in Kingston, it was such a relief!

Chris Blackwell was the producer of Lance's jazz albums (*"Lance Hayward at the Half Moon Hotel"* and *"Lance Hayward at the Half Moon Volume 2"*), and I was featured on these. The first album featured Ernest Ranglin on guitar along with Frankie Rabain. Lance played the piano and led on the vocals, whilst I played the drums and Maxwell Smith played the bass guitar. We recorded a compilation of nine songs, on this album. Some examples of the tracks were, *Ocho Rios, Begin the Beguine, Ethiopia, Streets Where You Live,* and *All the Things You Are.* The tracks on the second album included, *This Could Be the Start of Something, Old Devil Moon, Love Me Tender, Montego Bay* and *Dancing on the Ceiling.*

The extent of our hard work was less evident in the first album (*"Lance Hayward at the Half Moon Hotel"*). The quality, and sound was poor in comparison to what we had heard in the studio and we were so disappointed! It is possible that Chris had used a cheaper vinyl to reduce cost, but this speculation did nothing to ease our feelings. We felt more positive about the production of the second album, (*"Lance Hayward at Half Moon - Volume 2"*), which was of a much better quality. One of the reported musical write-ups, relating to its release in the 1960s, acknowledged "Lance Hayward as Chris Blackwell's first discovery". The reporter also complimented talented Bermudian jazz musicians, and to my amazement, listed me (Clarence Tootsie Bean), as one of those talented Bermudian, jazz musicians, together with the likes of trombonist Iris Burgess and saxophonist Clifford Darrell.

For this second album, singer Totlyn Jackson joined the band to do some of the vocals. Totlyn was a black, Jamaican jazz singer with an excellent voice. Lance had heard her perform in a nightclub and right then, and there, he fell in love with her voice and asked her to join the band. Totlyn sang in all the nightclubs we performed at in Montego Bay, except for the Half Moon Hotel and she did a brilliant job. Hearing her excellent rendition of the song *"Old Devil Moon"* on Lance's album, was simply amazing. Totlyn possessed a lovely, agreeable personality, so it was always a pleasure working with her.

In 1961 I was the featured drummer on Ernest Ranglin album, *"Guitar in Ernest"*, recorded with his band members (The Ernest Raglan Trio), and produced by Chris Blackwell in Jamaica at Island Records. Putting aside the mishap with Lance's first album, these recordings with Chris was honestly a lot of fun. I regarded Chris as one of those flamboyant, happy-go-lucky people, because that was just how he presented himself. What I really liked about him was the fact that despite his managerial position, most of the time he behaved as if he didn't have a care in the world; and I began to think that perhaps this was just one of the features that success brings.

I would usually spend three or four seasons annually, (including the winter months), touring Jamaica with Lance's band, before returning to Bermuda on time for the summer, music gigs, when there was more work for jazz musicians of our calibre. Bermuda was a popular destination for students during the *"College Weeks"*. This was a period, during the spring, when college students from various US states, and other countries, came to Bermuda for a month, to celebrate the spring break. Most of them resided at the Elbow Beach Hotel, and some people will remember, the influx of students, who were drinking, dancing, socialising, and doing whatever else they had a mind to do on the beaches and streets during those times. These students supported the organised beach parties, as well as outdoor and indoor events that provided much work for local musicians.

Lance Hayward, Milt Robinson, Maxwell Smith and I, were featured performers at some of these College Weeks. We spent hours entertaining the students in the hot sun, at the organised beach functions and a few other venues. Totlyn Jackson had accompanied our return to Bermuda on one occasion, and stayed throughout our summer season gigs. During this time, we also supported her performances at the Jungle Room and the Windsor Hotel.

Bermuda used to host many events in those days. One of these prominent events was the annual Bermuda Festival launched in 1976, jointly organised by violinist, Lord Yehudi Menuhin, Sir Edwin Leather (the former Bermuda Governor) and John Ellison. Lance and I performed at this festival in 1979 with singer LaVerne Haywood, and an overseas trumpet player. It was pleasing to know that several people in the community felt this type of event was appreciated, and very exciting to host on a small island like Bermuda.

I had a great time performing in Bermuda and Jamaica with Lance Hayward, but things were about to change for us. At the age of fifty in 1966, having decided that it was time for a change, Lance migrated to the USA and this was a great loss to Bermuda. No need to ask, I missed him greatly, but as life would have it, we were destined to meet again some years later in New York, where Lance had continued his career as a pianist.

When we did eventually meet up in the States, one of our highlights was Chris Blackwell's invitation to perform at a London venue with all expenses paid, and of course we gladly accepted. We knew that apart from performing, the other pleasurable aspect, would be meeting up with Chris again after all those years. This was my first time performing in London, so the venue's name and location, are a vague imprint in my mind. What made our performance special, was the fact that Lance and I knew just how to perform to engage an audience, and as we complemented each other on stage, our talent and skills were well noted.

Lance Hayward will be mentioned at several points in this book, because he played such an important part in my life and career. It is important to acknowledge that in the years we had worked together he had taught me many things to improve my skills, and aid my survival. Lance's son, Stuart reported in an article, that his father migrated to the States, because, as quoted, "he viewed his life in Bermuda as one big struggle against the prejudices of the sighted". I would also like to add here that Lance migrated to the

States at a time when foreign musicians were more favoured in Bermuda, so it is my belief that he sought new avenues to gain more recognition.

Lance spent the latter part of his years residing in Manhattan, where he died from pneumonia at the age of seventy-five, on the 9th November 1991. At Lance's funeral, I was invited to pay tribute to his memory, and due to being so distraught, regrettably I could not find the strength or the utterance, to honour him in his passing. Yet it is a surety that I will always remember this great musician, and recall our time performing together with the fondest memories.

Tootsie Bean, Lance Hayward, Totlyn Jackson and other band members.
Photo: Courtesy of Music on the Rock by Dale Butler

Photos courtesy of Music on the Rock by Dale Butler

Tootsie Bean with Lance Hayward, Bryan and Cyndy Butterfield, Norman Astwood, Maxwell Smith and Totlyn Jackson.

Chapter 9: Sporting Days

Playing golf is something I had enjoyed for many years, even though initially, I never thought I would. I owed this pleasure to guitarist Frankie Rabain, who sparked my interest in this sport during our time in Jamaica. Frankie was a skilled musician, as well as a skilled golfer. He played the sport regularly at Port Royal Golf Club in Bermuda, and in between our performances at a golf club in Montego Bay. Reportedly, he had won the *"Bermuda Open"* on two occasions in the 1970s and was the first Bermudian to qualify and play at the *"Open Championship"*.

Despite Frankie's rated talents, driving a car was a skill that he did not possess at the time we worked together, so I took on the task of driving him to the golf club, and waiting long periods in between, before driving him back to our hotel. It was during one of these waiting periods that Frankie decided to give me some unexpected advice that placed golfing on my agenda. I specifically remembered him saying, 'Tootsie, you drive me here all the time and wait for me to finish playing golf. Instead of just waiting, why don't you learn to play the game, so that we can play it together.'

At the time, I had no understanding of how to play golf, and absolutely no interest in playing this drawn-out sport. Yet thinking about Frankie's suggestion, learning to play it, seemed like a better way to spend my time at the club. Eventually, I gave in to the enticement and surprisingly made steady progress, with Frankie Rabain, who became the president of the Bermuda Professional Golfers Association, as my first instructor. With his encouragement, I took further lessons with a professional golfer in Bermuda, and after a while, there was no turning back. Playing the sport and swinging that golf club, became plain sailing for me!

It took a while, but with regular practice, I became a skilled golfer (very much like a pro), and went on to be a competitor in many Bermudian golf tournaments. In December 1987 for example, to my credit, I scored a hole-in-one at the 18th hole of the Castle Harbour Golf Club, (now the Tuckers Point Hotel), and gained a certificate for this achievement. As my love for the sport grew, I played golf whenever or, wherever I could, including during the time I resided in the USA.

I remember turning up once at the popular Watts/Willowbrook Golf Course in Hollywood, buzzing to play the sport, only to find out from the manager that a tournament was about to take place. Under normally circumstances, I would have walked away disappointed, but when he mentioned the word "tournament" I was all ears! My voice must have projected an element of excitement when I said, 'Really! I would love, to compete in this tournament!'

I had made this statement on impulse with a speck of optimism, so when the manager confirmed that I was eligible to be a competitor, pending payment of the registration fee; I knew it had to be my lucky day. Paying the fee was not a problem, except for the fact that my wallet was at the hotel and there was no time to fetch it, however I was about to discover that being acquainted with famous people, had its advantages -for real! Luckily, there was a spectator there, who recognised me as one of Ruth Brown's musicians. He stepped forward and offered to pay the fee on my behalf, with one condition, I had to promise to pay him back that night, when he attended Ruth's jazz concert, at the Hollywood Boulevard nightclub. Participating in that tournament was the most important thing on my mind at that moment, so putting my principles aside, I accepted the offer. Besides, paying him back that night would not be a problem. I would definitely be there, on stage, seated right behind my drums!

The Ninth Annual "Watts and Willowbrook Golf Tournament" that I was excited to be a part of, was organised for golfers of all age groups, and I could feel the excitement building up, even though there was a seed of doubt about the possibility of actually winning. Putting my doubts aside, I allowed my determination to kick in and then made the decision to take the game in my stride, perform at my best, and be satisfied with the outcome, regardless! This tournament happened many years ago, but what will always be remembered is the surprise and delight I felt, winning second prize from amongst all those competitors; and being presented with the trophy that is still proudly displayed in my cabinet to this day.

In case you are wondering that night, during the show, the man who kindly paid my registration fee, turned up at the club to collect his money as agreed, and judging by the smile on his face, I suspected that he had thoroughly enjoyed the show.

The other type of sports that I loved, and had learned with much practice to play skilfully, were table tennis and lawn tennis. At the start of my lawn tennis years, I was performing six nights a week and would sleep for only a few hours before, rising to go to the tennis court. The fact that I was getting very little sleep inevitably led to tiredness, and with it, feelings of ill health, but nothing could make me stop playing expect a firm warning from my doctor. He said, 'Mr Bean, if you want to stay healthy, you will either have to give up drumming, lawn tennis or whatever! Because, you cannot be working nights and then talking about going to play tennis afterwards, with very little rest!'

My doctor was right, so there was no point arguing. Tennis is a very strenuous sport, so proper rest to generate the stamina to play and endure the game, especially in the Bermudian heat, was vital. There was no way on earth though that I would give up my music, to pursue sports, so I had to make a firm decision to either give up tennis or, continue playing and suffer the consequences. In the end, I believe I chose the right option.

Frankie Rabain

Chapter 10: Johnny McAteer

After Lance left Bermuda, I sought other jazz bands to perform with to continue doing what I loved doing most. The reputable and very professional, Johnny McAteer Society Orchestra" was very popular then, with regular performances at the Inverurie Hotel, next to Darrell Wharf in Warwick. I was aware that working with such a popular band would ensure a regular income, but I also knew that things could get kind of "ticklish" (which was simply my way of describing it), when it came to securing a job with Johnny McAteer. Most Bermudian musicians knew that Johnny McAteer had made it very clear he would never hire local musicians to play in his band. His reasons for this were very vague. Assumingly, he felt most Bermudian musicians lacked music theory knowledge, or he might have had another reason.

When Johnny McAteer's drummer was about to get married, he contacted me to request cover, and due to my preference for being constantly in demand, I agreed. To my mind, I had performed with some of the best bands on the Island, so being a replacement drummer for Johnny McAteer's band was no more of a challenge. From my calculation, Johnny must have held me in high regard after this performance, because despite his reservations about hiring Bermudian musicians, when his drummer left the band in 1968, he hired me as a replacement.

Throughout the years performing with his band, Johnny McAteer never failed to make it known that I was the first local musician to perform on his bandstand, and I didn't have a clue, why he had a change of heart! At a guess, it could have been my reputation, or the fact that I could read music like other local musicians, who had learned music theory. The ability to read music was very important for the band. Johnny had singers, dancers etc. arriving in Bermuda every fortnight from the USA, Hawaii, and other countries for his shows, so having this skill was necessary to cope with the frequent rehearsals and subsequent performances. Thanks to Winslow Fox, my music theory skills were more than adequate, so I fitted in nicely with the band during these rehearsals.

The musicians in the Johnny McAteer's four-piece Orchestra were sax player Sid Katz, upright bass player Harry Millen and me as the sole drummer. Johnny was the pianist, singer and bandleader, and he always led the band to play the latest tunes. Now, I do not consider myself as much of a singer, but I liked singing. At times, I would do some singing with Johnny during the shows, which I believed was pleasing to the ear of the listeners.

Overall, the time spent performing as a member of Johnny McAteer's band was both rewarding and pleasurable. Johnny and bass player Harry Millen shared my golf interests, and we played this sport, whenever it was conveniently possible. We also shared a good business relationship. The paid vacation benefits for example, was much appreciated. No bandleader I had worked with previously, offered, or could afford to give their band members paid vacations - not even Lance Hayward. Adding to this, we had one important thing in common that we both shared - our date of birth! This was a date that we treated as special, and would celebrate together each year with a bottle of champagne.

My performance with the Johnny McAteer Orchestra at the Inverurie Hotel lasted for eleven years. This was the last band I was professionally associated with in Bermuda before migrating to the USA. When I finally decided to leave the band, evidently, neither Johnny nor Harry Millen wanted me to leave. I remember Johnny saying, 'Tootsie, you don't really want to leave do you?'

Thinking back now, maybe I had mixed feelings. Perhaps a part of me was sorry to leave this great band, and this conflicted with the fact that I felt it was time to move on. After all, as the saying goes, "the only thing constant is change".

Johnny obviously needed to recruit another skilled drummer for my replacement, but when the time came to do so, apparently, he reverted to his old way of thinking. Despite all we had been through professionally, he was still adamant that he was not going to hire another Bermudian drummer, and I was not having that! Not after all the time I had invested in his band. I had wondered then, if he had not learnt anything to change his former perception, given the years spent performing with a Bermudian musician that he personally viewed as a skilled, competent, good-natured drummer.

My plan was to introduce Johnny to a skilled drummer that I could vouch for as a replacement, and Eddie Ming was my ideal choice. In my opinion, he was an excellent drummer. In fact, Eddie was not just any drummer; he was someone that I had taught and one of my previous, talented students. Before introducing him to Johnny, I had informed Eddie of everything he needed to know, to perform in the Johnny McAteer's band. All that was required afterwards was for Johnny to look beyond his prior perceptions, and view Eddie as the skilled drummer that he was.

Although I had a good feeling about the outcome, it was hard to predict, how Johnny would respond to Eddie as a possible replacement. However, as it turned out, there was no need to be concerned, because surprisingly, he really liked him. Johnny offered Eddie the position and welcomed the fact that he was quite adept at reading music, so my plan had worked! With the problem solved, I left feeling very pleased that a skilled, Bermudian drummer had taken my place in Johnny McAteer's band. A band, which up until that point, with me being the exception, had never performed with a Bermudian drummer, especially one from the black community.

Eddie is now known as, Professor Eddie Ming, and amongst other activities, currently teaches drum lessons in his studio in St Georges. Reflecting on this replacement tale, leaves me with the thought that at the time of joining Johnny McAteer's band, Eddie Ming, as musicians often say, certainly had his "ducks in a row!"

Old photo of The Johnny MaAteer Orchestra with Tootsie Bean

Chapter 11: Calypso Trio

Jazz was always my passion, but even so, my strive to be flexible, meant increasing my skills to a level where I could play the drums professionally, to any type of genre including calypso. As historically recorded, calypso music originated in Trinidad and Tobago with strong African roots, and its popularity extended all over the Caribbean and Bermuda, between the 1940s and 1950s.

When I toured Jamaica with Lance Hayward, the calypso bands and singers we observed gave me the idea to do the same for a short while, and funnily enough, there was a period in my career where I did just that. My repertoire included performances with the Al Harris Calypso band, The Four Deuces calypso group, and calypso singer Sidney Bean and his band. Not to exclude calypso musicians like Hubert Smith, the Coral Islanders, the Talbot Brothers and Limbo Dancer Winkie Tatem. Let me just say here that Winkie Tatem was great! When he did the Cocktail Shake dance, he had this amazing ability to skillfully balance a tray of drinks on his head, without spilling a drop of the contents.

At one point in my career, I joined forces with guitarist Milt (Milton) Robinson and bass player Maxwell Smith to form, the Calypso Trio band. We coined the band's name to reflect what it would represent, and the name speaks for itself - three band musicians performing calypso music, aimed at an audience interested in this genre. Playing the drums to jazz music was my preference, but the music scene was changing, so easing out of my comfort zone (even if it was just for a while), seemed like a good thing to do. We created the band at that time, because we believed it would be a profitable venture that might also give us the opportunity to tour other Caribbean islands.

My most memorable time with the Calypso Trio band was our performances at the Elbow Beach Hotel, where many other musicians, for example Hubert Smith, had performed. We were contracted to deliver special performances for the Champagne Breakfast Initiative, aimed at honeymoon couples, as they dined and sipped champagne, and had enjoyed doing this mainly because there were no complications attached. We also had the additional option of performing to the hotel guests, leisurely soaking up the sun by the swimming pool.

Occasionally during a performance, some influential promoter would be present in the audience, seeking to offer bands like ours, the opportunity to perform overseas. On one occasion, we just happened to be in the right place at the right time to be approached for this. There we were, performing on the beach, without realising, we had an observer; and that the opportunity to perform overseas was just a handshake away. When the promoter made himself known, with an offer to perform at a nightclub in the Bahamas, we were so excited. This was something we were hoping would happen, and we could not wait to get on that plane.

We flew to the beautiful island of The Bahamas, with all expenses paid, to perform at the selected venue, and I have to say that the support from the audience was uplifting. They loved our music so much, they could not stop dancing or, perhaps I should say they could not stop whining up to the calypso beat. Whether or not they had rhythm made no difference, because that, in itself made the trip special. We did notice at some point that strangely, there were no signs of the locals we expected to attend; and later learned that apparently in those days, tourists were the main supporters of nightclub performances. We had no idea why this was the case. There were rumours about the barring of locals from some venues but, even if this was factual, it was still great performing to a full audience that were foreigners just like us.

The Calypso Trio band lasted a few years and had served its purpose during that time. Undeniably, it was a pleasure working with Milt Robinson and Maxwell Smith, during the lifespan of the band, because they were amongst the very skilled, professional musicians for whom I had great admiration. As mentioned in a Royal Gazette interview, the musicians I had worked with over the years had a lot of talent and were sincere and impressive. Thinking back on those days, I feel indebted to those musicians, who gave me ideas on how "I should do this, and not do that!" In other words, how things should be done, or not done to succeed.

The Calypso Trio. Maxwell Smith, Tootsie Bean and Milt Robinson
(Photo courtesy of Music on the Rock by Dale Butler).

Photo Courtesy: of Dale Butler

Tootsie Bean, Sheila Smith and other musicians

Photos courtesy of Dale Butler.

Chapter 12: My Teaching Days

Lance Hayward and I had recognised the musical talent in Bermuda's youths before he left Bermuda, along with the fact that there were no avenue for these talented young people to nuture and fulfil their potential to become professional musicians. We both felt that music would give these young people a sense of belonging, and help to maintain their focus to remain on a straight path.

After I returned from training in the USA, in addition to performing and taking on additionl jobs to supplement my income, I decided to offer tutoring to give something back to my community. My aim was to offer drumming lessons to compensate for the lack of facility in schools and in the process, produce skilled, local drummers. During that period, there were a number of young men on the Island, who had expressed an interest in playing the drums. I was fortunate to have had the opportunity to teach many of those youths, and to proudly observe the progression of those that had followed in my footsteps, to become skilled dummers or tutors.

The Bermuda Musicians Club, situated in Joell's Arcade on Angle Street, in Hamilton, was where it all began. This old building near the Catholic Church had the potential to accommodate what I had in mind, and was the first premises chosen for my planned tutoring. Using jackhammers and other tools, it took a while for my friends and I to excavate, and transform the basement into a suitable, habitable space. Once renovated, it also served as a musician club, where people could hang out and listen to various band performances. My lessons were delivered there for a period, before relocating to a rented studio at the top of the hill, on North Street, opposite the Transport Control Department. This studio then became the final base, where I taught drumming lessons to young people seeking my tutelage, for a small fee.

Additionally, I had volunteered my time for a short while as a Teaching Assistant at the old Bermuda Technical Institute in Prospect. Working alongside Track and Field Teacher Mr Longe, I taught students to play percussion instruments in the school band, and it was pleasing to see the positive results. With Mr Longe's permission, I led the school band on one occasion, steering the students, who had developed a liking for my style of teaching, into doing a great preformance, and this was one of the highlights of my time there. The students were very receptive, and evidently, eager to grasp whatever they were taught, so undoubtedly my efforts were well spent. Mr Longe proved to be a good, inspiring teacher, and it was my hope that his students would make good use of the skills taught in future years.

◀▶

All my tutees had showed respect for the tutoring received, and over the years have thanked me many times for the skills gained. Some commented that I had taught them skills that many of their acquaintances were unaware of at the time. Percussion Teacher Kevin Maybury, drummer Nick Swan and Professor Eddie Ming mentioned before, where just some of the people I patiently taught in their younger years, and had encouraged to use their talent and strive for perfection. Some of my students pursued other career paths, or responded to a higher calling, but had still found my teachings or acquaintance beneficial.

When I met the Reverend at my church for example, I had failed to recognise him at first, and the realisation afterwards that he had been one of my students, came as a pleasant surprise; especially as he was now declaring the love of the Lord to all. There were other young people, who although I may not have taught them directly, had benefited from my free advice and response to their questions. One example is my friend and jazz musician, Nathan (Nate) Lucas, who I had met through his father Maxwell (Max the Sax) Lucas.

To Nathan, I was one of Bermuda's treasures. He had mentioned my "encouraging manner" in a Royal Gazette news article, together with the fact that "he had learnt a lot from just being around me". Earlier on in his career, older, inspiring musicians did not have the patience, or the time of day to respond to his questions and some were usually dismissive. However, in a heart-felt, comment that I very much appreciated, he stated that, "this was not the case with Tootsie, who always found the time to give me an answer". The most important thing he would never forget about me, he said, was that I always had time for youngsters.

Working with other musicians and teaching my skills to young, potential drummers, highlighted the fact that I wasn't the only person, who started out beating drum rhythms on anything I could find within my home. Many accomplished musicians and youths starting out, did something similar. Jeron Clemendor, a Berkeley Institute student who received a scholarship in my name, ("The Clarence (Tootsie) Bean Scholarship"), in December 2012, was one such young man, who started playing drum rhythms on pots and pans at a very young age. Jeron had heard me playing the drums at church, and was inspired by my style of drumming. As publicised in a BDA Life article, Jeron had apsirations to become a professional drummer, or a music teacher, and it was therfore an honour to present him with a $1,500 cheque, in acknowledgement of his musical achievements and excellence.

Music Teacher John Woolridge, felt Jeron was rightly awarded, given the fact that he was one of Berkeley's exceptional students. Mr Woolridge appreciatively commented that, "being a musician and a performer, he is one to wish for the days when you could go out and hear the likes of Tootsie Bean". In his opinion, I was "one of the Island's musical legends," and knowing that the scholarship was awarded in my honour truly thrilled hs heart.

It is worth acknowledging here that the scholarship funds were raised from *"The Joys are Flowing Gospel Jazz Concert",* hosted by my church (The Heard Chapel AME). The Award Ceremony also featured fellow musicians and performers such as Toni Robinson, saxophonist Keith Lee and the Apex Four.

I gave up my tutoring and studio, before migrating to the States and gratefully, my son Shelton took on the task of teaching some of my students. Noting how some of them have progressed makes me feel proud for sure, because they are a living testimony of how music can positively change lives.

When asked the question, 'Do you believe that music can help young people in this day and age?' I definitely had to say, 'yes, but distraction is a problem!' Years ago, if a young person were taking music lessons, apart from their education that is what they would mainly do, and that's where they would focus their energies. Nowadays, there are too many distractions in the home, and community, that only serves to hinder their progress, whilst on the path to fulfilling their potential.

Chapter 13: The Music of Today

The writer of this book had asked my opinion about the music of today, and although it is not my desire to be overly critical of producers or musicians, in my view most of the music I hear nowadays, is just all rhythm! Lance Hayward as most people know, was my bossom buddy, and he had emphasied the fact that "there are three elements in music - melody, harmony and rhythm". When muscians are producing music, it should really encompass all three elements, and there are times when I question if this is always the case. From what I have noticed, there is hardly any melody to some of the modern music aired today - it's just all rhythm!

It has been said that what most people tend to remember about a song is the melody, more so than the actual lyrics. In the past, the melody in the music was the thing - it was at the forefront! A song always had a melody that meant something, but now, like Lance and I had discussed before, everything is about rhythm, and I feel so disappointed that music has taken such a turn. Some of the songs recorded now, have no story to the overall production of the music, which is the lyrics and the music combined, and most of the lyrics, is repetitive. You will hear the same lyrics over and over again, which to my mind, lacks imagination and creativity.

Another point I would like to make is that in modern day drumming, there is a lot of emphasis on the heavy bass. Sometimes when I listen to young people playing music in their cars, all I can hear is this heavy bass blaring out of the window, and similar to the lyrics, the same drum beat is consistently repeated. To give you an example, some years ago, I met up with a band from the states that used to play the hill billy type of music and we all went to the Splash Festival, where a number of groups were performing. Returning home, I mentioned to my son Shelton that, for every group stepping onto to the stage to perform, the drummer had the same excessively, loud introduction - a rupputum tum, a rupputum tum, bap … bap … bap! There was no variety!

When it comes to performances, some drummers avoid using the brushes that is supposed to soften the sound. In my heyday, playing with various bands, I avoided playing the drums hard, and would use the brushes to soften the drum sound and accompany the performer, especially if they were singing a softer tune. Playing an instrument above a performer to the point where the audience can't even hear the words being sung, is a growing trend. The importance of doing this is something that I just can't comprehend. With the exception of one artist that will be mention later, any performer supported throughout my musical career, would confirm that they loved the way I played the drums, because I accompanied them, instead of over powering their performance.

I strongly believe that the drums should be played to accompany the performer. That is the correct thing to do …well at least it was in my time! Like I had often told my past students, 'The drums are supposed to be felt and not just heard,' especially in the way it is played today. I am also reminded here of a statement I once made to a reporter in the States, 'The role of the drums is in the rhythm, while the bass keeps time!'

It's very likely that some musicians might disagree with the sentiments outlined in this chapter. They might wonder what the fuss is all about, and even suggest that we just have to move on with the times. Well …I suppose from the evidence around us, it is very clear to see that modern drummers and their fans have done just that!

Chapter 14: Family Life

I was still residing with my sister Erminie and contributing financially to the household income, before I migrated to the USA. Whilst doing my band performances, I also sold Sweet Pea flowers on Front Street that my sister had packaged to add to our finances. During my earlier years of performing, as mentioned previously, I took on additional jobs to supplement my income, one of which was a driving position, doing deliveries for the Bermuda Bakery.

Working for the Bakery was a stroke of luck, because this is where I met my lovely, wife Stella, who was an employee of the company. At the time of the writing this book, we had been happily married for sixty-five years. She supported my decision to pursue a music career over the years; selflessly compromising at times to allow me to pursue opportunities that would further my interests, to ensure I would have no regrets in the future.

Stella and I have three children, Deborah, Donna and Shelton. In addition, I have my daughter Jeanette from a previous relationship, and several grandchildren that we all love dearly. We are both very proud of all their achievements, and I believe that they are equally proud of mine. Donna now holds a prominent position with the Bermuda Athletic Association. She furthered her education in the USA after completing secondary education at the Berkeley Institute, where she was in the "Gold House" and part of the Berkeley Institute Sports Hall of Fame, Athletics Class of 1975. She was also Bermuda's top middle-distance runner at the time. Most recently (19th October 2018), we were very proud to attend a ceremony held in honour of Donna's induction into the Berkeley Sports Hall of Fame, for her outstanding service to athletics.

Deborah showed signs of a musical interest in her earlier years. She had learnt to play the piano, and displayed an interest in playing the drums. I had visions of her becoming the first female drummer in Bermuda, which unfortunately did not happen. I am not sure if Deborah regrets this more than I do, but I am mindful of the fact that in this life, we must all find our own path and interests. Jeannette and I have remained very close, and over the years, we have both cherished the times spent communicating with each other, as well as all our planned, special lunch dates that were equally valued.

My children have always liked to hear me perform on or off stage, or at concerts, so I felt very pleased when Donna organised and promoted *"A Night of Jazz"* concert at the Berkeley Institute Auditorium, in November 2006. She had arranged this purely to obtain the satisfaction of seeing me, and her equally, talented brother Shelton perform together to an audience. This turned out to be a very special event in the community. And, judging by the response of the supporters, the "Shelton Bean Quintet" with Bob Sanger, Joe Robinson, Jason Foureman and Melva Houston, and the "Tootsie Bean Quartet, with saxophonist Jerry Weldon, organist Akiko Tsuruga and guitarist Milt Robinson, did a fantastic performance.

Out of all my children, my son Shelton is the only one, who has followed, in my footsteps and because of this, I felt it necessary to acknowledge some of his achievements in this book. Shelton had shown interest and the potential to be a good drummer from a young age. When he began banging my old drumsticks, on things around the house, this reminded me of what I used to do years ago, so I knew that he was a drummer in the making. I clearly remembered purchasing a pull-cart for his Christmas present one year, and was taken aback when he seriously said, 'I don't want this … I want a set of drums!'

At the time, purchasing a set of drums was out of the question, but I made sure to do that after he graduated. As they say, "No pain, no gain!" Shelton attended the Berkeley Institute in Bermuda, before progressing to Berklee College of Music in Boston, where he had first class tutoring from skilled, drumming tutors such as Keith Copeland, Alan Dawson and Gary Chaffe. I thought it best for him to study at Berklee, because these reputable teachers, had the means to produce excellent drummers, which was just what he was aspiring to be. Completing additional training to gain competence in music theory was also a valued addition to his skills.

To tell the truth, initially I thought about discouraging Shelton from pursuing a career as a drummer; simply because some parents were having second thoughts about encouraging their children to make music their livelihood, and I was leaning towards that type of thinking. The competitive nature of the music industry, and the unsurety of earning a wage to make a decent living, did not make things any easier. However, once I began to realise that under my tutelage, Shelton showed the aptitude and potential to succeed as a great drummer, I gave up on the idea of discouraging him. He had perfectly, executing everything taught about drumming and turned out to be one of my star pupils.

One of his achievements was performing with the Ghandi Burgess Orchestra, along with the international musicians that Ghandi brought to Bermuda to perform at Southampton and Hamilton Princess Hotels. Shelton's repertoire included performances with Melba Moore, Freda Payne, Vanessa Ruben, Marlena Shaw and Melva Houston in the US. As well as, the Joe Wiley Band, and the *"Bermuda Is Another World Show"*. In the States, Shelton toured with several bands, performed regularly with accomplished musicians, such as Bob Sanger and Joe Robinson. He was also featured on their albums, and on that of upright bass player Jason Foureman.

In February 2013, Shelton and I were both guests on a Bermuda radio show. When the host asked Shelton to explain what he had learned from me as a musician, his response was, as quoted, "I had learned to be humble and honest - an audience will always know when you have given your all". Shelton also expressed the view that, "It is important for young people to be true to music," and those who have the desire to pursue a career in this field, "should work hard and go for it!"

In his teaching role at the Bermuda School of Music, Shelton is in an ideal position to influence and inspire such students to achieve, whilst doing his part to promote music positively in schools. I firmly believe that in these modern times, this type of influence is essential for the youths in our community, and I feel proud of my son's contribution to the future of these youths.

Father and son (Shelton Bean and Tootsie Bean)

Chapter 15: Migrating

By the 1960s, local musicians were having to face the situation once again, were venues and hotels had begun to hire more foreign musicians. Consequently, some had difficulty obtaining work, and were forced to consider overseas tours. Some succumbed to performing at social engagements held at churches, parties, halls etc., or leant alternatively towards rebranding themselves as "Entertainers" rather than musicians. For a few others, it was time to think seriously about the option of migrating, in search of new opportunities.

Initially, the idea to migrate was partly driven by a personal, lifelong desire that started some years before. My brother-in-law Maxwell had all the latest vinyl records and I had spent some time listening to the different drummers in his collection, three of which I thought were exceptionally talented. The first drummer from among Maxwell's collection that impressed me, was the jazz and swing music drummer and bandleader, Chick Webb (William Henry "Chick" Webb). Second on my list was drummer, Papa Jo Jones (Jonathan David Samuel Jones), who was part of the Count Basie Orchestra in the earlier years and labelled in his time, as the greatest drummer that ever lived. Third in line was drummer and composer Gene Krupa.

When it dawned on me that these were all American musicians, who had developed their skills in a country that produced great drummers, I became preoccupied with the thought of performing someday, with these talented, musicians. In fact, this was the main reason, why it was always in my heart to travel to the States, but first, I needed to deal with some necessary matters. Being a responsible father, I had put my migration plans on hold, because I felt it was important to wait until my children, had completed their education.

◄►

I arrived in the USA in 1979, feeling optimistic, and excited about the possibility of fulfilling my dreams, in the country where jazz originated. As discovered shortly after my arrival, obtaining a green card legally was a difficult process that would take time, the extent of which was hard to determine. This card was a necessity to gain the right to remain and work in the country, and as I realised then, it would have probably been easier, if I had applied for it before entering the country. Lance Hayward had migrated to the US prior to my arrival, and as he also found the process of obtaining this card problematic, it was obvious that I would experience the same.

Had it not been for my wife's sister, Olive May, the situation might have never been resolved. Luckily, before Olive left Bermuda, she had married an American with a similar name to mine (Clarence Countryman), and he had sponsored Stella to obtain her Green Card. Being that Stella was my wife and legally in possession of this, eventually I managed to get mine off the back of hers and this was such a relief! Now I could work and move on to the next stage of life in the US without worrying about immigration.

I migrated to the States ahead of my wife Stella, who followed once the authorities had issued her Green Card. Stella secured a part time job in a dental surgery in a relatively short space of time, and was doing her best to settle in this foreign environment. She gradually grew to like America to some extent and was adjusting to the cold weather, as well as the novelty of seeing the snow and travelling via the subway to get to work.

Despite Stella's efforts to settle in the US for five and a half years, in the end, she was really missing our home and family in Bermuda. "Home is where the heart is", as the saying goes, so when Stella decided to return home, although I would miss her greatly, I had to respect her decision. Nevertheless, returning home to see her and my family in Bermuda as often as possible in the years that followed, offered some compensation.

Chapter 16: Forging My Way

There was no doubt that jazz was one of the great loves of my life ever since I can remember. My desire to obtain more exposure in the jazz field, along with the urge to be right there in the centre of things, where it was all happening, were the other important factors fuelling my desire to migrate. Fortunately, for me, migrating allowed the opportunity to meet and perform with some of those musicians that were my inspiration. I felt like I was living my dream and this was a great feeling for someone like me, who came from such humble beginnings.

Living and performing in New York I believed, brought out the best in me in terms of my skills. The range of skilled musicians, young and old, residing there that I could observe, were far more than I had anticipated. Some were renown musicians, in the seventies age bracket, but still on top of their game. Apparently, at one point, jazz and blues appeared to be phasing out in popularity, but now this genre was making a comeback, and live entertainment performed by jazz and blues bands were attracting fans on a large scale. Being there, at that time, I could see there were many opportunities to express and transcend my skills to the next level of professionalism.

When Rock and Roll became popular, the nightclubs hired black, American groups to perform. To me, this was my opportunity to watch and learn from these highly, skilled drummers, because you can never stop learning in an ever-evolving music world. I was also astute enough to grasp every opportunity to learn new techniques when it came my way, and equally, some of those US drummers, might have learned a few techniques from me.

In the early stages of my relocation to America, Lance did his best to assist me in whichever way he could. We decided to work together for a while, performing in nightclubs, but not to the extent that we had performed before in Bermuda and Jamaica. Lance had secured a contract as a solo pianist at a venue called The Village, in downtown New York. During this time, he had also formed the "Lance Hayward Singers Chorus". There was a saying by fellow musicians, that when Lance opened a show, "he would never miss a beat". Funnily enough, some of the musicians I had performed with, attached a similar reference to me - "Tootsie never missed a beat!"

In my quest to find more work in the US, Lance took me to all the nightclubs in town and introduced me to various bandleaders, who he hoped would give me a chance to perform in their bands, but there was so much competition. Many musicians would persistently hang around venues like the Eddie Condon Night Club, hoping to obtain gigs. Also, most musicians, had names of other skilled professionals in their "little black book" that could perform when needed, as their replacement, and being new on the scene, I knew I was missing out! I did have some faith though that, once I had the opportunity to prove my skills, it would only be a matter of time before my name would feature in their little black book. My only hope was that it would not take too long to manifest.

Most of the bandleaders that Lance approached on my behalf were hesitant to offer the opportunity to perform, because they had no knowledge of my repertoire or my skills. When Lance introduced me by name, some of them would say, 'Tootsie who!'

This was understandable to some extent, because it was unheard of for replacement musicians of any particular skills, to just walk onto a bandstand expecting to perform. Bandleaders selected replacements, firstly by known reputation, or by recommendation from a reliable source. Lance however, never gave up. He persistently targeted and pestered these bandleaders as if he were a flea in their ear, until finally …finally, one of them conceded! This bandleader gave in either because he was fed up of Lance's pestering, or was desperate enough to give me the break I so badly needed.

I remembered making my way up to the bandstand, to begin playing with band members, I had never met before, and this brought back memories of my debut performance at thirteen. The only difference this time was that I had several years' experience under my belt, and my nerves were well contained. Knowing that the eyes of all the band members were on me, I gave it my all, making sure my performance was tight to complement the rest of the band and in the end, despite my general, modest persona, I have to say that based on that performance that, is when history was made! Lance informed me afterwards that a man from the audience said to him, 'That drummer is a fraud …no one from Bermuda can play the drums like that!'

From that night onwards, my name was in several black books. There were so many cover requests from drummers, unable to commit to their scheduled gig, that I found it hard to keep up and recall all their names. What I do remember however, is the fact that my performance met every band challenge. I therefore rapidly earned recognition as the skilled, talented drummer from Bermuda that could blend in seamlessly, with any American band requesting my services.

Bandleader and organist, Jon Hammond from San Francisco, hired me for a short while for his jazz band, and this had the added benefit of getting me more exposure. I met Jon by chance whilst performing in a Broadway nightclub, and he immediately requested my services. Jon travelled frequently, so on average he only contacted me when he secured a gig, and needed a drummer, to join the other members of his four-piece band; guitarist Matt Smith and saxophonist Brett Ryan. These were all skilled, amicable musicians, and we certainly had a lot of fun performing together while it lasted.

Cleopatra Needle Restaurant, on West 92nd Street in Broadway, was one of the main venues for Jon's gigs. This was a well-known venue, with designated areas for a bandstand and dinning, so that our supporters could dine and be entertained at the same time. These "Jazz Buffs" as they were labelled, loved jazz, and would regularly support our performances, come rain, come shine! Apart from the occasional band performances, I did not have much more to do with Jon or his band members, so it was only a matter of time before we lost contact with each other, and went our separate ways.

With so many requests to play the drums, after a while, I was performing almost every night. Due to my late working hours, it was difficult for Stella to attend most of my gigs, but she made every effort to attend those labelled as special performances, despite her dislike for those loud, band mikes. As mentioned before, Stella was homesick, and all these factors combined inevitably led to her decision to return home, whilst I remained in the US, to continue seeking and accomplishing what was foremost in my mind, when I migrated there.

Tootsie Never Missed a Beat!

Jon Hammond on the organ.

Chapter 17: Earle Warren & The Countsmen Band

Duke Ellington, (Edward Kennedy Ellington), was a musician that I respected. To have had the opportunity to perform with this great jazz pianist, composer, and orchestra leader, would have been a dream, but the only way this could have happened, was if I had the chance to meet him in person. Duke Ellington had taken ill some years before he was due to perform in Bermuda, and had passed away before my arrival in the States.

I did have the opportunity however, to meet the "Count" himself. Count Basie (William James Basie), jazz pianist, organist, composer and bandleader - was another famous musician that I admired. Lance Hayward and I had met him during one of his band performances at a US nightclub, prior to his death, and that was truly a great show. The "Count" had a reputation for being very professional, and his style of music was the type I enjoyed as a lover of jazz. As much as I would have liked it to be, performing with Count Basie wasn't one of my achievements. Instead, I had performed with the famous Countsmen band, founded, and led by Earle Warren, with some of the original musicians of the Count Basie Orchestra.

Up until the 1950s, musician Earle Warren was a first lead, alto saxophonist, and singer, in the original Count Basie Orchestra. In 1972, Earle formed the six-piece Countsmen band that critics regarded as a "classic swinging big band" and very "Basie-oriented". In his musical career, Earle had performed at jazz festivals and on The Sound of Jazz television show. Incidentally, Earle Warren and I had first met in Bermuda through a fellow musician, who had introduced me simply as "Tootsie", and although he might have heard of my surname, "Bean", the name "Tootsie" was what he remembered.

When his drummer requested my service, he informed Earle that a drummer by the name of "Bean" would be replacing him in the show. As the story goes, Earle was not pleased to hear about arrangements for a sit-in drummer without any prior discussion, especially since up until that point, he had never heard of a drummer called "Bean". Arriving at the venue as agreed, it only took a glance, for Earl to recall our meeting in Bermuda, where at the time, he had rated my drumming skills highly. When he saw me, the look on his face was priceless as he exclaimed, 'Ahh! It's Tootsie!

Having such a welcome from Earle, with expressed recognition for my skills, lifted my spirits and reassured his band musicians of my competence. Shortly after my first performance with The Countsmen band, fortunately for me, the drummer resigned, and Earle recruited me as his replacement. I accepted the position without hesitation, because, as a matter of fact, I had enjoyed performing with Earle, and knew the popularity of the band, would ensure the exposure that I sought.

Earle Warren and I, along with pianist Don Coates, bass player Jimmy Lewis and trombonist Eddie Durham, worked well together. We performed at various venues, particularly those, on Uptown 42nd Street, in Times Square, known for its grand theatres. I was also the featured drummer on Earle Warren's recordings produced in between our performances. Wherever we performed, The Countsmen band enjoyed the popularity along with the good reviews from critics. I felt honoured, every now and again, to note articles about our performances, with some reference to my skills. Reporter John S. Wilson's for example, drew comparisons between the Count Basie Orchestra and The Countsmen band, in which he had stated that, "with Don Coates on the piano and Tootsie Bean on the drums, The Countsmen band, is a properly swinging representative of the Basie tradition".

The Countsmen band dismantled in 1992 to the dismay of all the musicians. Two years later, we learned that Earle Warren had died at the age of seventy-nine, reportedly from complications of a stroke and kidney failure". I suspected that Earle had dismantled the band due to his age, and failing health that most of us knew very little about. Yet the band members he had left behind, including me, respected him greatly, and will remember him as one of those great musicians of his era.

Earle Warren

Chapter 18: Bobby Forrester & Irene Reid

I had met Organist Bobby Forester in 1979 shortly after migrating to the States and for some reason we just clicked in terms of the way we interacted and never looked back. When we met, Bobby had been working on and off with singer Irene Reid and her band. He had grown up in the Bronx where he began playing the piano from the age of nine, and was a trained classical pianist, guitarist, and an excellent organist. Rhythm and Blues was Bobby's first attraction, before he branched off into jazz, and was further influenced, by the likes of the great Charlie Parker and Dizzy Gillespie.

After we met, Bobby Forrester and I performed at various gigs with many skilled musicians - Billy Mitchell, Turk Mauro, Harold Vic, C. I. Williams, Jimmy Witherspoon, and most frequently with tenor saxophonist Harold Ousley. We had also recorded an album with jazz saxophonist Frank Wess. There were times when in addition to supporting Irene Reid; we promoted and performed at our own gigs, as the *"Bobby Tootsie Duo"*. Some of our performances were with the late Gwen Cleveland, whom I met through Harold Ousley, at the Uptown venue in Brooklyn Avenue. Gwen performed at jazz concerts on Long Island, and Sonny's Night Club. From my recollection, she was an excellent blues vocalist, with a very fiery nature. She flew off the handle fast, mind you, and did not take any nonsense from anyone.

When Bobby and I performed together, our talents never went unnoticed and were often, reported in news articles, which in effect boosted our popularity. These write-ups on our performances were always complimentary. I was graciously aware of my skills, enriched through various band performances; yet as a newcomer to the States, the overwhelming recognition and comments received from fellow musicians and US reporters, never failed to surprise me.

For instance, US jazz music reporter, Stuart Troup commented on my "gentle, soft-spoken manner" together with the suggestion that once seated around a drum kit, I became "a dynamo at playing the drums". My energy as he described was, "a match for Forrester" not to speak of the fact that we "feed and enriched each other, with metaphors and currents". Reports like these would normally boost any musician's morale, and I was no exception. The only difference was the fact that I modestly attributed such recognition to my continued hard work and God-given talent.

Meeting famous jazz singer, Irene Reid from Savannah Georgia, was purely through my acquaintance with her drummer, Clyde Lucas, who just happened to be a friend of mine. Irene began her career singing in high school and church, before moving to New York, where she had a spell performing with the Count Basie Orchestra that propelled her to fame. Both Clyde and Irene's trumpet player, Jonah Jones (Robert Elliot Jones), had met me previously in Bermuda, during my performing years with the Johnny McAteer Band. At the time, Jonah had forsaken his commitment to perform with Irene Reid in Germany, to travel to Bermuda with Clyde, who apparently wanted to assist me. Whenever Clyde visited my homeland, he would always say, 'Tootsie, anytime you come to the States, I will definitely hook you up with some musicians.'

Now when I think of it, with the exception of Irene Reid, I don't think he ever did! Clyde was aware that my skills had been in demand in Bermuda, and was similarly in demand in the USA. So with this in mind, he requested my services as his replacement for Irene's gig in Germany. The returned airline ticket he forwarded, supposedly, was meant to ensure that I had the means to travel and would no doubt turn up for the gig. The unexpected opportunity to perform in Germany, with all expenses paid, courtesy of Clyde and Irene was enticing, and one that I had no intention of missing. Yet, I knew that travelling to Germany would be a new experience, and having never met, or performed with Irene, it was hard to predict what I would encounter on arrival, in this foreign country.

Considering all things, I thought it best to put my concerns aside, which was a good thing, because Irene would have belittled me with just one statement, if I had allowed her so-called welcoming words to affect me. When I met Irene, she looked me up and down, critically assessing me on first impressions, before brazenly saying, (with all the body language attached), 'Well…I don't know … I used to perform with a drummer called Clyde, and now he sends me this boy called Tootsie!'

The emphasis on the word "boy", definitely wasn't music to my ears! *Who exactly is this boy you are referring to?'* I should have asked, but of course, I was diplomatic and courteous enough to let this sentiment pass. Besides, I could not think of anything to say on the spur-of-the-moment that Irene Reid would not immediately view as confrontational … something I have always avoided with a passion throughout my career. On the other hand, knowing that when it comes to drumming, I would have no problems proving my worth or ability, I knew she would see the "boy" she had referred to previously, in a different light. It was just a matter of letting the drums do the talking!

My performance that night evidenced my professionalism and diminished any doubts or concerns that Irene initially had about my skills. Also, in Clyde's absence, she was very pleased to have me perform on the tour with the rest of the band (The Bobby Forrester Trio band). So, it was not surprising that after Clyde's resignation, I was Irene's first choice for a replacement drummer, working alongside, Bobby Forrester and baritone, saxophonist Turk Mauro. Sometimes when I played the drums and she was overly pleased with my performance, I could hear her shouting out, loud and clear, in the background, *'Alright!'* No doubt, all thoughts of the "boy" she had wrongly envisaged had evidently disappeared.

Unlike the USA, there were no problems with immigration when I performed with Irene in European countries, and later in Japan, because there were fewer restrictions. Earlier, when my Green Card was still in the processing stage, to avoid any issues resulting in deportation, I went back and forth at intervals to Bermuda, until I had it in my possession, and could legally reside and perform in the country.

Irene and Bobby's supporting band that I was now a part of, had performed at many venues in the States, including Sonny's Place Jazz Club in Long Island. Sonny's Place, was one of those popular clubs that jazz lovers liked to visit, and Count Basie was a frequent patron at our live performances there. We made appearances with Irene on several occasions at Mr Hicks Place (a venue in Roosevelt, New York), and at the Flamingo Cocktail Lounge in Brooklyn, (labelled as the *"Home of the Stars"),* where bands like the Harold Vick Quintet regularly performed. Another interesting event that we were featured at, was the anniversary of the Long Island Jam Festival, where we had a great time fuelling the energy of Irene's fans with our performance. Added to this list of memorable events, were similar performances at the Showman's Café, and on the Jazz Mobiles.

Apart from meeting Count Basie, one of my highlights performing with Irene's band, was meeting the famous guitarist, composer and Grammy Award winner, Earl Klugh, at a venue in Detroit. Earl Klugh, a musician ranked as one of the finest American acoustic guitar players, and one that I rated as an excellent guitarist with a "fine touch", entered the venue with his guitar and greeted us warmly. Then, unexpectedly, he stepped onto our bandstand and performed with us as an uninvited guest. It was such a pleasure being there, performing with him on stage. His spontaneous performance lived up to his reputation and added to the enjoyment of our fans, who I am sure thought they had experienced an unforgettable night of jazz.

I had fitted in seamlessly with Irene's band members, and we had all worked well together, which is something I could say about most bands, because I had the knack for getting on well with all sorts of people. Irene was highly regarded in the entertainment circles. Jazz festivals and various jazz venues, always promoted her in their adverts, featuring Bobby Forrester and I, as part of her supporting musicians. The headlines often depicted her as "Sensational", "The High Priestess of Soul", "The Dynamo of Sound", or "The Entertainers Entertainer", which were accurate descriptions of her as a performer.

I would also describe Irene as a very skilled and talented jazz singer that was "picky" in her preferences, because, strangely enough, unlike most musicians, Irene preferred performing to an audience at venues in poorer areas, as opposed to those in Downtown, New York. This preference led to our frequent performances at "The Strip", "Olga's Groovy Pub", "Small's Paradise", and other venues in her beloved Harlem. I have memories of her proclaiming proudly that she was, "The queen of the ghetto!" and I honestly believed that she really meant it!

Bobby Forrester's band had backed many musicians and singers, performing at one of the jazz nightclubs that we frequently performed at with Irene - the name of which I choose not to mention here. Some of these musicians were dabbling in drugs, obtained either off, or on the premises. They were often so spaced out that, at the end of their performances, they would forget all about collecting their pay. Given that this club was located right next to a police station, it was strange seeing what went on there on a regular basis. What I found puzzling was the fact that police officers had never visited the premises whilst this was going on …well none that I was aware of any way! If they were there undercover, to my knowledge, they had never once made themselves known, or given any indication that they suspected, or were even aware of what was happening on the premises. Without a deterrent, it was no wonder that the drug situation continued throughout our frequent gigs, and perhaps even long after our performances there ended.

I made many visits to Bermuda, whilst living in the States, which kept me abreast with the entertainment scene there. One of the big attractions in Bermuda during that time was the *"Charlie Bascombe Show"*, hosted by promoter Charlie Bascombe. Mr Bascombe arranged for musicians from different parts of the world to perform in his show that was a good stage for exposure. Bobby Forester and I had performed in Charlie's Show before, with Milt Robinson, sax player Gerry Weldon and jazz singer Gita Blakeney. Charlie learned about the US musicians from our interaction, so when Bobby and Irene accompanied me on a trip to Bermuda, he grasped the opportunity to feature Irene in his show, at the Galaxy venue on Pittsbay Road. She was supported by Bobby, sax player Billy Phipps, and guitarist Calvin Dove, and her performances were so great that Charlie invited her to do an extra week of performances, which she declined, due to her pending commitments in Harlem.

Irene Reid had benefited greatly from the support of a fan base that had grown significantly during her performing years. Assumingly, they along with her surviving, supporting musicians of many years, were saddened to hear about her passing, on the 4th January 2008, due to a cardiac arrest. I was in Bermuda at the time and after hearing this news, I confess that my feelings amounted to the same.

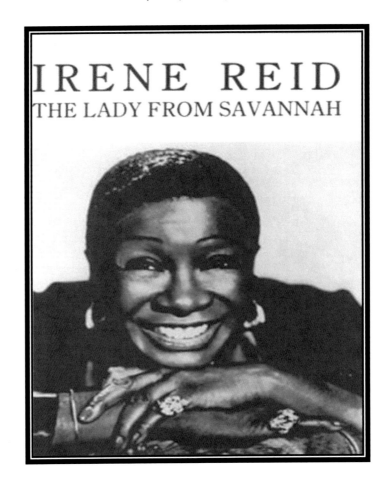

Chapter 19: Ruth Brown

Over the years, the number of famous, remarkable musicians and vocalists that I had performed with for a short or lengthy duration, exceeded my expectations, and my repertoire has since served to evidence the fulfilment of most of my aspirations. Irene Reid and Ruth Brown, (both of whom have since been laid to rest), are at the top of my list of great vocalists, and I am thankful to have had the opportunity to support such talented singers.

Most of my travels as a drummer in the States took place when I performed with Ruth Brown (Ruth Alston Brown), who the press labelled in 1991 as the real R&B Queen. I had met Ruth initially through organist Bobby Forrester, at the Showman's Café, whilst we were both performing with Irene Reid. Ruth was a well-known singer with a fantastic, powerful voice that was similar to Irene's. Her innovative ability to add a pop music style to rhythm and blues songs had a great impact on the music scene for many years. Ruth's recording contract with Atlantic Records in the 1950s, earned her several hit songs, including the song "Mama He Treats Your Daughter Mean" that propelled her to fame. She retired from the limelight in the 1960s to raise her family and returned to renewed fame earning a Grammy Award and Tony Award in 1989, for best female performer and for her albums *"Blues on Broadway"* and *"Black and Blue"*.

The opportunity to perform with Ruth's band was simply a stroke of luck that came my way whilst performing with Irene. I had accepted her drummer's cover request, because performing in Ruth's band was an opportunity of a lifetime that I could not miss. After all, this was none other than the famous Ruth Brown … a singer I had admired for many years. Walking onto Ruth Brown's bandstand as an unknown entity, it wasn't much of a surprise to encounter the same "welcome" received from other bands, when I arrived as a replacement drummer for the first time. I can still recall the scene from all those years ago, where her band musicians stood watching and silently questioning, as I suspect from the look on their faces, *'Who is this drummer?'* To them, I might have appeared reserved or unsure of myself, up until the point when I positioned myself behind the drum kit, and felt the adrenalin flowing through my veins.

The show began, and I could feel all eyes in my direction as I quickly got into gear, and eased into the rhythm to accompany the band. As we progressed, what surprised me the most was the atmosphere the band generated, and the tightness of our performance that I had no way of predicting; because surprisingly, we all clicked as if we had always played together as one. It was a feeling that is hard to put into words, but one indication of how I felt, was the smile on my face. Some of my acquaintances at times referred to me as "the drummer with the smile", so as you can imagine, my smile was probably bright enough to light up the room! I had no idea then that shortly after this performance; I would become a permanent fixture in Ruth's band, that in my eyes was looking so splendid on the designated bandstand.

Bobby Forester had previously performed with Ruth in Los Angeles, prior to performing with Irene's band in 1977. When Ruth met up with Bobby once again after my sit-in performance, she begged him to return to her band, and he did. By this time, Bobby and I were good friends. We knew how to work well together, so after Ruth's drummer resigned, Bobby wasted no time contacting me about the vacant position. Understandably, Irene Reid was annoyed when we both left her employment, but in our assessment, working for Ruth would prove to be a better option, and more beneficial for us in the long term.

Not many people knew that in my younger years, I had listened to Ruth Brown's excellent rendition of a song and had seen her perform. Listening to her fantastic vocals left me in awe of her talent, and this was the beginning of what some would call a teenage crush. As my talent and skills grew, so did my aspiration to perform with her, and now my dream was about to unfold before me. Funnily enough, when I eventually told Ruth, about the teenage crush, she was very amused, and embarrassingly I became the object of her teasing for quite a while. My teenage crush had obviously faded by the time I became a permanent member of her band, but what had always remained was the high level of respect I had for her vocal talent and performance that, was similar to the respect she had for me.

Ruth had planned several tours by the time I had joined her band. Her supporting Quintet: Bobby Forrester on the Hammond organ, alto saxophonist C.I. (Charles) Williams, tenor sax player William Bill Eastley, guitarist Bill Williams and finally me on the drums, were all skilled musicians and we made a great team! I interacted with Ruth's band members, in a similar way to other bands; the only difference was we knew just how to gel, and our performances always maintained that expected, professional standard. Ruth took us on tour to many places in the world, starting with tours right across America, including North Carolina. Although it was enjoyable for the most part, touring from State to State, and travelling to various gigs across the country (including down South) was hard, tiring, and scary.

In those days, racism was widespread, but more so in the South. Travelling to these parts of the country, even as famous musicians, we always had to be on our guard; never knowing if we might be attacked by the Ku Klux Clan or other crazy people, who did not want black folks in their area. To state that I was only a bit concerned venturing into these parts of the country was an understatement - I was very scared! My fears especially escalated, when Ruth told me about a few incidents that both her, and the band members had encountered. One such example was the time in the earlier years of her career, when someone literally threatened to shoot her during a performance.

The organiser had featured Ruth as the opening act, and as the main artist was running seriously late, she attempted to appease the audience by singing her popular hit song, *("Mama, he treats your daughter mean"),* a few times. Ok, I agree that no matter how good the song was, hearing it over, and over again, would have been too much for the audience to cope with, but this was no excuse for what took place next. Without warning, a man in the audience, who felt he had heard enough, rose from his seat, and walked right up to the edge of the stage with a gun in his hand. He placed the gun on the table in front of her, before saying threateningly, 'If you sing that song one more time, I'm gonna blow your head right off with this gun!'

Ruth did not reveal how she responded to this nerve-racking encounter, but at a guess, she must have felt extremely concerned when she saw him approaching the stage with the gun, and even more so, when she heard the threat. It is frightening to think about what might have happened if the man's threat had become a reality, because hat performance could have been her last!

On another occasion, when Ruth's band members were travelling on their tour bus to a performance, an armed County Sheriff pulled them over and demanded to know where they were going. Eying the Sheriff's gun was enough to make the band members do whatever he had ordered, because there was no telling what he would have done, if they had refused. The musicians confirmed they were on their way to perform at a gig and hoped that would be enough but it was not! The Sheriff's next question was about the type of instruments they all played. When they responded, he ordered them to take all the instruments out of the truck, which they did. He had a no-nonsense look on his face when he then said … wait for it, 'Now, play for me!'

There were times when Ruth fearfully anticipated friction between black and white supporters that could possibly wreck her performance, because in some areas, incidents such as this occurred at times, and encountering the opposite, sometimes came as a surprise. Witnessing the positive effects of the "clothesline divide" for the first time at a venue was quite a revelation. This clothesline, put in place to reduce racial tension, (minus the clothes pegs mind you!), stretched from one end of the room to the other, dividing Ruth's fans into two sections. Black folks were on one side and white folks on the other, but as she observed, these fans were dancing and enjoying the music to such an extent, there were no visible signs of racial animosity. One news reporter wrote that, "Music had proven to be the common denominator that brought all these ravers together", and having witnessed this, Ruth might have concluded the same.

As stated in a Royal Gazette interview, when I joined Ruth's band, one thing I did not expect to see was youths, who were not even born at the peak of Ruth's fame, twenty years ago, enjoying her songs. The audience at most of our performances were from the younger generation and surprisingly, they were not just standing there looking disinterested - they were really enjoying themselves, singing and dancing to her songs. I believe her appeal to such followers was possibly due to her style of music, which seemed to have transcended the gap between the youths and the more mature generation, and for her, this was quite an achievement.

Chapter 20: Celebrities, Festivals & TV shows

One of the things I liked about performing with Ruth's band was the fact that regardless of where we performed, Ruth would always ensure that we had the means to travel to the venues. If we were touring or performing overseas, Ruth would send us airline tickets to travel to wherever we had to go and would ensure that we were booked into the best hotels to enjoy our stay. Ruth's manager had employed a good strategy. He would promote her shows weeks before a performance, so by the time we arrived the tickets were sold out entirely, and the long line of fans could hardly wait for the show to start.

Although I had pursued a career as a drummer because of my love for the drums and jazz, as opposed to the celebrity status, when treated like a celebrity in the music world, despite my modesty, I must admit that it felt good! Sometimes Ruth would introduce us band members to famous people, who loved her performances and they in turn, gave us the celebrity treatment. There were also times, when performing with Ruth at certain events, had the added bonus of meeting celebrities, such as those I am about to mention.

I am sure most people have heard of Smokin Joe. Well, we were performing once at a venue, when the famous Joe Frazer (aka Smokin' Joe), who fought with the great Mohammed Ali, was in the audience. He was a fan of Ruth and had especially attended the show to see her perform. After the show, Joe met with Ruth and us band members, expressed his enjoyment for our performance, and to our amazement, invited us all to his house. I was of the opinion that we had to make our own way there, but then his shiny, limousine pulled up to escort us like important celebrities. The location of Joe's lovey abode slips my mind, but I do recall having a great time there. Joe cooked us a proper chef's meal and entertained us to the point where we could all "let our hair down", as the saying' goes, and have a good laugh.

When it was time to leave, we were transported home in his limousine, and relaxing in the luxurious back seat, I couldn't help thinking, *'This is the life!'* Normally when we toured or played out, I always had a camera in my possession, eager to click the button and capture the images of that passing moment. I had taken photos at Joe's house, to remember the occasion, but you can imagine my disappointment when all the processed photos were over exposed. Of all the times I had used my camera (at home, USA, Europe Japan etc.), this was the time it had to mess up on technicalities.

In July 1991, we turned up at an outdoor jazz event in Jacksonville, to perform with Ruth, only to find out that the famous actor and comedian Bill Cosby, was the celebrity host. Mr Cosby was his usual, comical self throughout. He had us all in fits of laughter, when he introduced the band, and announced that Ruth had asked him to play the drums, whilst she performed. We didn't have a clue, whether or not he had the skills to play the drums, but we knew he liked our performance, and maybe, if given the opportunity, he would have attempted to do so, if only to humour the crowd.

In the 1980s during one of our gigs at a venue called Green Street, in Greenwich Village, New York, who should walk in but the great, Stevie Wonder. It was one of those unexpected, welcomed moments, and to my mind, the only thing that would have heightened the mood, was if Stevie had decided to perform with the band. I have always respected Stevie's talent and contribution to the world of music, so it was interesting chatting with him in person, and even more so when he chose to reveal something about himself that none of us knew. Apparently, Stevie was a big fan of Ruth, who was in her sixties at the time and still going strong. He revealed that Ruth was the main source of his inspiration during his youth, which was probably before the start of his career. This surprising confession made me realise that we had something in common, and I could not help wondering then, if Stevie had also had a teenage crush on this great queen of R&B.

At the height of her popularity, Ruth had several publicity interviews with American TV talk show hosts that she normally concluded with a live performance to the delight of the audience. Ruth always had a yearning for performing on TV shows. She had watched the Johnny Carson's show since its first airing, wanting so much to make an appearance, and had almost resigned to thinking it would never happen, when she received an unexpected invitation. My appearance on *"The Johnny Carson's Tonight Show"* in 1990 was mainly as a representative of Ruth's band. This was the world's longest, running talk show, broadcasted from NBC Studios, at the Rockefeller Centre in New York. Performing live to an audience on TV with Ruth's band, with all those lights and cameras focusing on our every move, was an entirely new experience. For Ruth, this was also an achievement, because according to a reported article, performing on Johnny Carson's show "was one of her most elusive goals".

Wherever we performed, Ruth's fame always preceded her. We attracted the attention of her followers, and reporters, whether it was at a jazz festival, in a major concert hall like the Lincoln Centre, or a simple venue like Michael's Pub in New York. Ruth was often interviewed by news reporters and there were various news articles over the years that, positively rated both Ruth's and the band's performance, that I was proud to be a part of. Reported comments such as, "The Quintet backing Ruth Brown was a definite enhancement to her performance", and the "Quintet, deftly blends the instrumental with Ruth's vocals" were very uplifting compliments for us band members.

During my years with Ruth's band, I cannot recall her ever receiving a negative response or comment at any of her gigs, regardless of the type of crowd or venue. I had performed with Ruth at some well-known venues, like for example, the prestigious Carnegie Hall on 7th Avenue New York. This is a place where I had dreamt of performing and where classical and other musicians have performed for years. It is hard to recall the full details now, but I do remember taking photos as a memento, and feeling completely in awe of this significant building, with such a great ambience that would set the mood for any performance. I think my smile was probably a noticeably fixture on my face throughout the whole performance. Ruth wowed the audience with her vocals and rendition of her hit songs, and of course, they enjoyed her band music that complimented her performance as always.

The Italy and Sicily tours in 1992, and those tours in Germany, France, Japan, and England were very exciting, and I had similar feelings when we performed in England. In 1994, I supported Ruth twice at the famous Ronnie Scott's Jazz Club in Soho, (the heart of London) that attracted jazz lovers from all backgrounds. The following year in 1995, we performed at both branches of this jazz club, (London and Birmingham) that were buzzing with regular jazz supporters. Sometimes these supporters would queue up from the door of the club, to the end of the street to see us perform. For these folks, whether they were listening to a live band performance, or a DJ's selection of music, Ronnie Scott's Jazz club was a lovely, warm, and entertaining place to chill out, drink, dance and have a good time.

Ronnie Scott's, real name was Ronald Schatt. I learnt afterwards that the Queen awarded him an OBE in 1981 for his achievements in jazz, had we known this at the time, we would have addressed him by his proper title - "Sir Ronnie Scott". When we met Ronnie, at his London club, Ruth's son had replaced her previous manager that had passed away. Ronnie did appear to be very ill at the time, so it was not surprising to hear of his death in December 1996.

To my knowledge, Sir Ronnie Scott, was a pleasant English man with respect for his fellow musicians. Being a musician himself (a jazz saxophonist), he respected and treated both black and white musicians equally, without any form of discrimination. He frequently had skilled musicians performing in his clubs, and I was very pleased that he had no designated "back door entrance" for black musicians - we had endured enough of those days! Our stay at a posh hotel overlooking a park, in the club's vicinity was one of the highlights, and overall, we had a great time performing in London, known for its fish and chips and red double decker buses, and an even greater time doing live professional recordings there.

◀▶

Ruth successfully recorded a thirteen track jazz album ("*Ruth Brown Live in London*") in December 1994 during a live performance at Ronnie Scott's Club, featuring Bobby Forrester and me, along with C.I. Williams, and the new additions to the band - bass player Carline Ray, guitarist Gregory Skaff and tenor sax player Robert Kenmotsu. I want to mention here that when it comes to drawing a comparison or, assessing the quality of a production between a live recording and a studio recording, I would always opt for live recordings. In my opinion, the studio environment often prevented musicians from "opening up" in the way they would normally do when preforming live on stage, so this usually had some effect on the outcome.

Bobby and I were also featured on Ruth's album *"The Soul Survives"*, recorded live at the Blues Alley Club in Washington in 1982, along with Saxophonist Earl Swanson and guitarist Billy Butler. This album included a remix of her famous 1950s hit song, *"Mama He Treats Your Daughter Mean"* and *"Teardrops from My Eyes"*. We had another show there in that same year. The weather was so bad on the day that all our hopes of having a good turnout was dwindling fast. As the evening progressed, it was only when we peeked through the window before the show, and were pleasantly surprised that we realised what was happening outside. Despite the freezing temperatures, our committed fans were wrapped up snuggly outside in large numbers, as they queued up to purchase tickets. So, that night, we had an unexpected, record-breaking attendance - one that we were not about to forget in a hurry.

I had toured Japan briefly with Irene Reid, and again with Ruth in 1991; and was surprised to find that the Japanese were very jazz-minded. It was evident that they had been studying and practicing how to play jazz music, because their musicians could imitate most things that those skilled, black American musicians could do effortlessly. Throughout my career, I had practice frequently, to keep on top of my game, and be as good as, or perhaps even better than other experienced drummers, considered as my equal. Before a gig, I would always make sure that I "got my ducks in a row!" as C.I. Williams and other musicians used to say, to suggest that their equipment was all prepared, and lined up like ducks in a pond, ready for the show!

Ruth normally toured with two skilled sax players - tenor sax player Bill Weasley and Charles (C.I) Williams, who had toured many places with her. On the Japanese tour, no one had any inclination that Charles was unwell, until the night he collapsed from an aneurism, whilst performing on stage. Everyone was shocked when this occurred. A moment of panic ensued, before the realisation kicked in, and we all stopped to focus our attention on Charles. The Paramedics took Charles right off the bandstand and rushed him to the nearest hospital, were he was retained for four days after surgery.

Charles was lucky to survive. Apparently, the Japanese medics had used a very advanced method of surgery to save his life. When he returned to the USA and had further medical examinations, the medics confirmed they had never seen an operation like the one he had. We were all hoping there would be no further complications, but this was not to be. Charles collapsed once again in the USA, due to a second aneurism and this time, there was no way of saving him. As far as we were all concerned, Ruth's band had lost a very talented, sax player that she might never be able to replace.

Ruth had a contract to perform with the band, for at least a week's engagement, in every country that we toured, and luckily things usually went smoothly, because she would have probably hit the roof, if we had encountered any problems that seriously affected our gigs. At one point, we were booked to perform on a boat touring the Hudson River and on a cruise ship, travelling from the USA to Bermuda. I was really looking forward to the experience of performing on the cruise ship heading for my homeland, because I had plans to visit my family. What was pleasing was the fact that the cruisers had nothing better to do than to eat, drink, dance and be entertained, so our band was guaranteed a good turnout for all scheduled performances. The ship docked for two days in Hamilton, and during that time Ruth was very pleased to have had a visit from a Bermudian fan that had met her previously. This young woman kept the memento Ruth had given her then, and was waiting patiently on the docks for hours to see her idol once more.

I was featured to appear with Ruth's band at annual, jazz festivals. Some of which were in Italy, Germany and Tokyo in 1995, but most were in the USA, particularly in areas like New York, Atlanta, Virginia, Detroit and Washington. The Musician Union sponsored the festivals and arranged jazz mobiles, to transport musicians and their instruments. These festivals were free to the public with road closures in place, so regardless of the location they were sure to attract a crowd that could enjoy themselves safely. Performing with other musicians at these events were pleasurable, exciting times, because we would all get swept-up in the euphoria, present on each occasion.

Ruth's popularity led to performances at many other festivals. For example, the Playboy Jazz Festival, the Chicago and Sacramento Blues Festival, and the Long Beach Blues Festival in California - one of the largest blues festivals in the country, held usually on US Labor Day weekend. The annual Chicago Blues Festival, hosted by Chicago's Department of Cultural Affairs, featured three days of performances from renown favourites and up and coming blues musicians. We did two performances with Ruth for each event and received the usual response from the crowd on each occasion. Nothing makes you feel more gratified as a musician, like when the audience warms to your performance, sing along to the memorised lyrics, and applaud with such great enthusiasm

These were incredible events and I felt the same about some of our other gigs. However, I had never imagined myself performing with Ruth Brown at such an important, historical event, as President Clinton's, 1993 Presidential Inauguration celebration; held at the John F Kennedy Centre for the Performing Arts. As musicians, our task was to focus on performing a selection of songs, chosen for this type of event, and as far as that went, we did not disappoint - we made sure to perform to expectation and above. I felt that just being there performing to all those present, most of whom we had never had the chance to mingle with before, was a great feeling, worthy to be remembered.

Chapter 21: Bobby Forrester (Moving on!)

Bobby Forrester and I had performed with Ruth Brown for more than eleven years before things changed. Similar to when we worked with Irene, at times I would perform with Bobby Forrester's band, in New York venues, that extended our popularity and income. Bobby was the sort of person, who liked to engage in drinking and smoking. Sometimes this excessive habit would get him into trouble, and I would always go to his rescue. He was also the sort of person, who ever so often, felt the need to try something new. Knowing this made it less surprising, to learn that he had decided to part with Ruth's Band once again, to perform with other musicians. It is fair to say that I was disappointed, but as it was obvious that nothing, I could do or say would change his mind, I gave in and told him to go ahead and do as he had planned. In time, I felt sorry that he had not fared too well in his new venture, and perhaps this affected him more than most people realised.

Arriving home in New York late one night, I accessed a strange voice message on my phone. It sounded very much like Bobby's voice, but it was hard to make out what he was trying to say. The sound of his voice and unclearness of his message was a cause for concern, and my alarm bells were suddenly ringing. If I am not mistaken, I think I attempted to call him back, but had no response. To make matters worse, I had no knowledge of his new address to pay him a visit. The only possible action to take was to contact his mother to check up on him. Waiting for news from Bobby's mum left me fearing the worst. The next I heard; the medics had confirmed that Bobby had died alone in his house on the 23rd November 2002. This was devastating news that Bobby's family and I found hard to accept.

The possibility that Bobby might have called that night to reach out to me in his final hours, was a niggling thought in my mind that I could not shake. Listening to his voice mail, the thought had never crossed my mind that this would be the last time I would hear from my fellow musician and close friend. Under such circumstances, nothing could be done to reverse the situation, yet I knew that if it were possible, I would have reached out to assist him in any way I could.

At Bobby's funeral service, close acquaintances, and musicians, who admired him and loved his music, filled the room. Towards the end, as a special tribute, guitarist Mark Marino, bass guitarist David Jackson, saxophonist Jerry Weldon, along with me on the drums, performed some of Bobby's favourite songs. Irene Reid then topped it all with her touching rendition of the song, *"I'll Be Seeing You"*. Bobby's funeral was reportedly a "truly touching service and celebration of life". All the musicians who gathered in his honour, left the funeral "swinging" as the reporter described, and I wanted to believe that Bobby went off to the next stage of his existence doing exactly the same.

Bobby Forrester & Tootsie Bean after a show

Ruth Brown's band members. Bobby Forrester 2nd from left next to Tootsie Bean
(Photo from Mr Bean's collection)

Chapter 22: Ruth Brown Additions

The annual Washington Square Music Festival in Manhattan founded in 1953, and The Telluride Film Festival in Colorado, near the awesome San Juan Mountains, are just a few of the events not yet mentioned, where I had performed with Ruth Brown. Without going into much detail, the Washington Square Music Festival was a free open-air event, with a focus on live operatic, orchestral, and jazz music performances. In contrast, the annual Telluride Weekend Jazz Festival had live jazz performances as its main attraction that had appealed to jazz fans from all over the world since 1977.

In addition to her great vocals, Ruth was always quite the entertainer. These skills she possessed, coupled with the "A star" performance from us, as her supporting musicians, were the reasons why she appealed to a huge fan base that always supported our gigs, regardless of the weather or the venue. When we performed in such huge open-air environments, apart from the fact that we all loved playing our instruments, the stimulus was knowing that these fans were there supporting us throughout and singing along with the songs. I derived a certain amount of excitement from performing at these festivals that made me enjoy the moment. If you were to ask why this is, I would have to say that the type of crowd these festivals attracted, generated an exhilarating type of energy, felt by both them and the performers on stage.

The Smithsonian Institution (center for astrophysics) event in Washington DC, the huge Wolf Trap National Park summer events in Virginia, and the Hollywood Bowl - an amphitheatre in Hollywood Hills, California, were some of the other venues where we supported Ruth's performance. Ruth chose to do another live recording with us at Wolf Trap Park, in front of a vast number of supporters, who had flocked to see her, and other musicians perform. These supporters filled the complex, with a wave of excitement that added to the buzz felt recording live.

I remembered us doing a gig once at a place in the States, situated high up in the mountain, where the air was so thin, we were all finding it hard to breathe. I was seriously hoping that the situation would not escalate to the point where we would need to see a medic or be air lifted to a hospital. To make matters worse, the following day it rained so hard, we were forced to perform in a tent. It was surprising to see our supporting fans, sitting out in the pouring rain with their children, just waiting for the show to start. Some of these crazy, but devoted people were drunk, which might explain why, and some were having fun, sliding down the slopes in the mud. If I had given it much thought then, I would have possible swayed to the thinking that perhaps they were just making the best of a given situation, whilst waiting for the real fun to begin.

Out of all the outdoor venues that I performed at the Hollywood Bowl was the most impressive. Its beautiful arches and scenic view of the Hollywood Hills was a remarkable sight, and the featured musicians, including us, drew a great crowd. I also remember performing with Ruth at a place called the "Bermuda Onion Night Club" in Canada, and on first sight, I had to take a step back to get a second glance and question, '*What's going on here!*' Now I know that us Bermudians can all draw cultural reference to the name *"Bermuda Onion"* and the origins behind it, but seriously … who, would expect to find a place so far away from home, with such familiarity in its branding.

Ruth along with rhythm and blues singer, Delores LaVerne Baker, known for hits such as, *"Tweddle Dee"* and *"I cried a tear"* in the 1950s, were the longest tenured Atlantic Record acts. With this Tenure came the entitlement for Ruth to be one of the featured performing artists at Atlantic Records 40th Anniversary Celebration, at Madison Square Garden, in May 1988 that, attracted R&B, pop and other fans. I performed with her band at this publicised concert dubbed, *"It's Only Rock and Roll"*. The line-up of well-known featured artists was impressive: Rufus Thomas and the Spinners, Ben E King, Roberta Flack, Wilson Picket, Booker T. Jones, Phil Collins, Led Zeppelin, the Bee Gees and more. This list of famous featured artists, along with the promotional strategy to include USA and UK radio and TV networks, ensured the success of the event.

When I realised that Ruth and us band members were to be featured in this celebration amongst those famous artists, I was thrilled to the bone. News of the celebration attracted people from all over the country and beyond. The celebrations began on the 14th of May and continued non-stop to the following day - a full thirteen hours of performance! The thrill of it all, created a wonderful atmosphere that I was excited to be a part of, and if I were only focusing on doing an A-Star band performance before, this occasion would warrant more. This celebration was one of the events my wife Stella chose to attend, in support of my performance, and surprisingly, managed to cope with the deafening sound of the amplifiers. As usual, Ruth's manager ensured we were all booked into a hotel in the city and after the long hours of performing, this welcoming perk felt like heaven. In fact, whenever I got the chance to experience a stay in this type of accommodation, it always made me feel like I was "living the life!" as the saying goes.

I had thoroughly enjoyed the time spent working as Ruth's drummer and performing with the rest of the band, but after eleven years, I clearly felt that the end of an era was rapidly approaching. Some months after Bobby Forrester's resignation, I too decided to move on to pastures new, and chose not to perform with Ruth again, possibly because the band was missing a particular organist that, I had held as a dear friend. As far as I knew, Ruth continued performing for some years, until it was time to move on. When legendary groups like the Beatles came on the scene, they became an exciting novelty, and in time, as forewarned in the music industry, talented singers such as Ruth Brown, gradually faded out of popularity.

Ruth Brown died in Las Vegas Hospital from a heart attack and stroke, in November 2006, at the age of seventy-eight. By then, in addition to being an accomplished singer of different genres, she had also risen to fame as a songwriter and actress. Ruth and I had worked extremely well professionally, showing respect for each other's talent. The opportunity she provided for her band members to tour and perform widely had many personal benefits. Most importantly, it enriched my cultural and musical experience and for this, I will be forever grateful to such a talented legend.

Young Ruth Brown

Ruth Brown's Album "The Soul Survives"
<u>**Credits:**</u> *Earl Swanson – saxophone, Billy Butler – guitar,*
Bobby Forrester – organ, <u>Tootsie Bean – drums.</u>

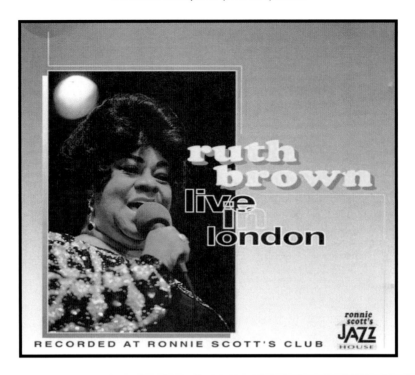

Ruth Brown's Album featuring Tootsie Bean (Clarence Bean)

Tootsie Bean on Japan Tour - (Photos from Mr Bean's collection)

Chapter 23: Moving On

After my work with Ruth's Band ended, Irene Reid requested my services again, and I worked with her for a while before moving on to play the drums for a few notable musicians, some of whom were well-known female artists. For instance, Carol Sudhalter, a jazz vocalist and highly respected saxophonist performing in a big band, Dakota Staton, who rose to fame with her 1957 hit, *"The Late, Late Show"*, and the famous Etta James, who had worked with saxophonist, and record producer, Houston Person, were just some of the female artists I had supported.

Etta was a beautiful person with a beautiful voice, and an admirable ability to sing different genres - jazz, R&B, gospel and even rock and roll. She was best known for her famous signature song *"At Last"* and other hits like, *"I'd Rather Go Blind"*, *"Don't Go to Strangers"* and *"Save Your Love for Me"*. I had met Etta when I was just settling into life in New York and working with Irene Reid. When we met, there were regular Sunday concerts in Harlem, featuring Irene Reid and Etta James on the same Billboard, and Etta's name was always up there in neon lights.

Just like Irene and Ruth, performing with Etta or, sharing a bandstand with her, was really something to rave about. Her unique vocals and performances were just great, which made playing the drums to her renditions an added pleasure. Etta and I became good friends in the end, and I loved her as such. When supporting her I was spot on with my drum beats, and always ended the performance on a high - a good one mind you!

Singer Sandra Reaves-Phillips from South Carolina was another female vocalist that I had performed with at a few concerts. We had worked well together, but as mentioned to a radio talk show host, she was the first singer I performed with, who specifically wanted me to play the drums hard …and I mean, real, hard! Sandra always liked to hear the drum beat upfront during her performances, and she would sometimes say, 'Tootsie - I want to hear that beat!'

Sandra's previous drummer's large hands, perhaps prevented him from playing softer beats. When he played the drums, regardless of the type of music, you could hear the beat thumping out right up to the roof. I have never liked playing the drums hard to override a performer, as most of my acquaintances will confirm, but on the other hand, if a performer wanted to hear the drums played hard, I would play it hard, simply because, they are the boss; and that was the case with Sandra!

American teenage jazz and blues Singer Helen Humes, a previous vocalist in Count Basie's band, arranged through Earle Warren, was another artist that I performed with. Some people saw Helen as a saucy R&B diva, with the skills to do a mature rendition of most popular songs, and that was my opinion when I performed with her. I also thought that for her age and experience at the time, she had developed a relatively good voice.

My repertoire included performances for a short while, with American blues and jazz singer Carrie Louise Smith. From what I knew of her, she had fans across Europe and very little popularity in the States, but overall, I had rated her as a good vocalist, on a similar line to Ann Hamilton Calloway.

US jazz singer, songwriter and actress, Ann Hamilton Calloway, who wrote and sang the theme song for the TV series *"The Nanny"*, had a preference for jazz, and rock and roll music. She was very pleasant to work with. One of the things I enjoyed about working with Ann that had no relevance to her performance, was sharing her flight. When Ann's manager had her scheduled to perform at a venue, he would send a private plane for her transportation and I always loved travelling on this plane, because despite its size, it was very plush, with all the comforts to ensure a relaxing flight.

If I were to sum up my experience performing with all these female singers, I would have to say that with the exception of Etta James, as talented and famous as they were in their own right, it was hard to compare them with the likes of Ruth Brown, Irene Reid and Totlyn Jackson, because in my honest opinion, these females were all such talented, legendary outstanding singers.

I was thrilled to have met American blues singer, guitarist, songwriter, and record producer, B.B. King (Riley B. King), who also had strong links with Etta James in her younger years. B.B. King was an excellent guitarist, whose style of playing had influenced many blues musicians. When he played the guitar, instead of using the steel bar, he would use his fingers to do something peculiar on the strings that in effect, created a unique sound. When I met B.B. King, I was performing at a few gigs that I had lined up, and it was on one of these occasions that the opportunity arose to share the same bandstand with him. In a similar situation to Count Basie, I did not have the opportunity to perform with B.B. King per se. Sharing the bandstand was regrettably the closest I had come to being his drummer.

BB King, had invited Ruth Brown on his tour. She was recovering from a hip operation at the time, so touring would have been too much of an ordeal, but I had often wondered if I would have had the chance to perform with him, had the situation been different. Apparently, rumour has it that B.B. King was very good to his band musicians. When he was at the top of his game, making good money, he treated them all to a house of their own. If this rumour is true, you could say that, not having the chance to be a member of his band had significant consequences - I would have loved to be on the receiving end of such a treat.

Jazz trumpeter, singer, and bandleader Doc Cheatham (Adolphus Anthony Cheatham), was one of the best jazz trumpet players of his era. I had performed with him once before his passing, but this was enough to gain his appreciation. Doc's decision to hire me was due to my circulated, drumming reputation, and this was clearly to his advantage, because my drumming complimented his performance.

I was the featured drummer on the documentary, *"That Rhythm, Those Blues"*, portraying Rhythm and Blues music, between the 1940s to the early 1950s. This showed footage of interviews with producers, and performances by major R&B singers of that era, including Ruth Brown. Similarly, American blues singer, Bobby "Blue" Band (Robert Calvin Bland) and I, were featured on the soundtracks of the 1988 film, *"Bright Lights and Big City"*, starring Michael J Fox, and directed by James Bridges. Unavoidably, we had to use sheet music throughout, so my music theory skills came in handy.

The time spent working on these soundtracks, recording music separately from the dialogue, was short lived in comparison to my other performances. In brief, this involved doing recorded performances to accompany, and synchronise with the documentary and film images. It was an interesting process, but not as exciting as envisaged, because I was basically hidden away in a studio, playing the drums to accompany other musicians. As for the filming, this was out of bounds! I had missed out, on all the film-set action, but overall, the experience was a welcomed addition to my repertoire.

Performing in nightclubs was unavoidable, and something I did frequently whilst working in the States and previously in Bermuda. In the US, this gave me the opportunity to meet and work with a few celebrities from the music, and performing arts industry. To support these celebrities, normally my selection would be from a known bandleader or, by recommendation from another acquaintance. Playing with supporting bands at these shows, as expected, the need to be flexible and sufficiently skilled to play any type of selected music, was paramount, to support the star of the show. When the curtains rose, all eyes would be on the star, performing at centre stage, and the standard of the backing music had to be on or above par.

Tap dancer Charles Honi Coles, who appeared in the film Dirty Dancing and Jimmy Slyde, were two of the performers that I supported. Jimmy was very popular in the US where he earned the title "King of Slides" due to his innovative style of tap dancing. His reputation as a tap dancer was never in question, but his ambition to revise tap dancing using the style of the great Bill Bojangles, might have been.

One of the other entertainers that I had the pleasure to support was American dancer, actor, singer, and choreographer, Gregory Hines (Gregory Oliver Hines), from New York, who is sadly no longer around. Gregory had studied dance, and his outstanding skills were easily observed in his tap dancing, comparable (if not more so), to the likes of Fred Astaire, Bojangles and Sammy Davis Junior that I had met on one occasion. Some people might remember Gregory tap dancing in the film *"The Cotton Club" or "The Gregory Hines Show"*, and that he did a duet with Luther Vandross. Gregory was one of those charismatic dancers with the ability to mesmerise an audience whenever he performed; and that was the case on the night, I supported his performance. After the show, I was pleased that he was happy to pose for a photo, to show his appreciation for my support. He was a great performer, and I only wish I could recall more about his performance on the night, to add to this chapter.

The spectacular Lincoln Centre in New York was a popular venue back in the day, where a range of classical vocalist and jazz bands performed, including Andy Farber's Orchestra. In 1985, I was part of the Andy Farber's seventeen-piece Orchestra, performing in an exciting tribute to the great Count Basie at the Lincoln Centre. We had an audience that were fans of both Count Basie's and Andy Farber's music, and had shared the bandstand with other featured, jazz musicians. This venue with its lovely ambience, was an attraction for many people, because of the simple fact that they were either lovers of jazz or classical music.

Bandleader and skilled pianist Felix Endico, led a very popular, swing dance revival band, called "Felix and The Cats". I had accompanied Felix and his band members on many concert tours across the USA, playing the drums to ballroom dance music, smartly dress in tuxedos. Felix was the star soloist in the band that was said to be a "hotter, looser, and more bluesy" type of swing music that was, "burning up the dance floor" and that is just how it appeared at times.

Wherever we performed, the place was always swinging with young people, dressed in zoot suits, or the long skirts and ankle socks associated with the rock and roll trend, as they danced, and sweated profusely from the swing fever. Sometimes the whole thing seemed a bit wild, but apart from the enjoyment of playing the drums, I had the most fun watching them prancing around, using an excessive amount of energy that some folks could never dream of doing.

Tootsie Bean and Gregory Hines after a peformance.

Tootsie Bean and Sammy Davis Junior (Photos from Mr Bean's collection).

More examples of other musicians included in my repertoire:

♦Clark Virgil Terry Jr:	A swing and bebop trumpeter and composer. Clark performed for a decade with Count Basie, Duke Ellington, Quincy Jones, and on the Tonight Show band.
♦Bill Doggett (William Ballard Doggett):	Jazz and R&B pianist and organist, who wrote the song compositions for "Honky Tonk" and "Hippy Dippy" and had performed with Johnny Otis and Ella Fitzgerald.
♦George Coleman (George Edward Coleman):	Jazz saxophonist an NEA Jazz Master, whose performance history included, Miles Davis and Herbie Hancock.
♦Lionel Hampton:	Jazz vibraphonist, pianist, percussionist, bandleader and actor. Lionel shared a history with, jazz musicians Benny Goodman, Buddy Rich, Charlie Parker and Quincy Jones.
♦Al Grey:	Jazz trombonist that had performed with the Count Basie Orchestra.
♦Charles Brown:	A blues singer and pianist famous for hit songs "Driftin' Blues" and "Merry Christmas Baby".
♦Little Jimmy Scott (James Victor Scott):	Jazz vocalist known for his high counter tenor voice.
♦ Big Joe Turner:	A recognised blues singer from Missouri.
♦Ernie Andrews:	A previous member of the Harry James band and writer of his biggest hit, *"Soothe Me"*.
♦Jimmy Witherspoon:	Post war blues singer, said to bridge the worlds between blues and jazz. Jimmy did recordings for Atlantic records.
♦Frank Wess:	American jazz saxophonist who was a member of the Count Basie Band. I was Featured on his album with Bobby Forrester
♦Arthur Prysock Jr:	A Rhythm and Blues singer best known for his baritone voice, and live show performances.

Tootsie Never Missed a Beat!

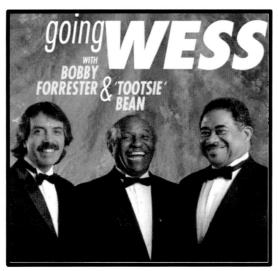

Jazz saxophonist, Frank Wess' Album, Featuring Bobby Forrester & Tootsie Bean

Title ▼	Performer	Written by	Info
Au Privave	Frank Wess with Bobby Forrester & Tootsie Bean	Charlie Parker	Originally by Charlie Parker and His Orchestra
Cotton Tail	Frank Wess with Bobby Forrester & Tootsie Bean	Duke Ellington	Originally by Duke Ellington and His Famous Orchestra
Crazy He Calls Me	Frank Wess with Bobby Forrester & Tootsie Bean	Bob Russell, Carl Sigman	Originally by Billie Holiday
Frankie and Johnny	Frank Wess with Bobby Forrester & Tootsie Bean	[Traditional]	Originally by The Leighton Brothers
I'll Never Smile Again	Frank Wess with Bobby Forrester & Tootsie Bean	Ruth Lowe	Originally by Percy Faith
Love Letters	Frank Wess with Bobby Forrester & Tootsie Bean	Edward Heyman, Victor Young	Originally by Dick Haymes
My Shining Hour	Frank Wess with Bobby Forrester & Tootsie Bean	Johnny Mercer, Harold Arlen	Originally by Glen Gray and The Casa Loma Orchestra - Vocal Chorus by Eugenie Baird
On the Street Where You Live	Frank Wess with Bobby Forrester & Tootsie Bean	Frederick Loewe, Alan Jay Lerner	Originally by John Michael King
The Lamp Is Low	Frank Wess with Bobby Forrester & Tootsie Bean	Maurice Ravel, Peter De Rose, Mitchell Parish, Bert Shefter	Originally by Andre Kostelanetz and His Orchestra, Kay Kyser and His Orchestra

Tootsie Bean at a concert / festival (Photo from Mr Bean's collection)

C J Symonds (Legendary Jazz radio host) and Tootsie Bean.

Chapter 24: My Ensemble at Pumpkins

Moving on permanently from the Ruth and Irene years, fortunately my reputation had preceded me, and thereby opened opportunities to perform and freelance, with musicians in parts of the States and other countries. After a while, I took on the responsibility of forming and managing my own band (*"The Tootsie Bean Ensemble"),* with tenor saxophonists Bill Saxton, Eric Wyatt, Mario Escalera and organist, Pat Bianca. They were all rated positively by critics and labelled by the press as Master Musicians.

My band did regular performances at some nightclubs, but my preference by far, was the popular Pumpkin's 60s Jazz Club on Nostrand Avenue, known as Brooklyn's number one premier jazz club and neighbourhood bar. Pumpkins Night Club was one of those venues that appealed to local jazz fans, who really loved and appreciated this style of music. When my band performed at Pumpkins, without the "big names" behind us to draw the fans, (Ruth Brown, Irene Reid the Countsmen etc.), it was important that we held our own, and we certainly did a good job of that. We warmed the crowd with our professional performances, and left them wanting for more every time we were featured there.

Regularly practice was necessary to sharpen our performance, to the point where we became, as reported, "a tight-knit band, where everyone seemed to understand exactly where their fellow musicians were at, during various stages of a performance". Other compliments, describing my band as "an awesome display, of one of America's greatest contributions to the world of Art and jazz culture", left of us all speechless. Equally impressive was reporter, Stephen Witt's critique of my performance that, I will share with you here. Despite the awareness of my own abilities, I have never had such compliments bestowed on me! I was "a risk-taking drumming master", according to Stephen, with a "flawless technique that kept listeners riveted to the sound". Not to speak of my "uncanny ability, to start off doing a rhythm, finding a general grove; then, effortlessly switching into another grove, or free-form drumming, whilst keeping the tempo even". If you are a drummer reading this, no need to ask, you will know exactly what all of this means.

My natural smile was something people often said lit up a room, and radiated throughout my performance on stage. Some of my relatives were of the same opinion, but in hindsight, maybe I should have accepted their compliments, and leave with the thought that perhaps, they were all a bit biased! I have taken this thing about my smile to another level in this book, because ironically, some people viewed it in a different light. The point I am getting at here, is that some folks took my so-called "beaming smile" as a testimony for drug taking. They thought I was grinning or smiling throughout entire performances, because something other than the music, (whether drugs or liquor), was making me "high". I should have really ignored these assumptions, because, how were they to know that my "highs", came purely from listening to the sound of the music I played, or from another musician's perfect performance.

If you remember, I had mentioned before about the drug use in a club, located next to a police station that I had witnessed on occasion as a non-participant. Without being judgemental, noticeably, some musicians appeared to be very "down in the dumps" at times. I had often attributed this to tiredness, and the hard life musicians experienced now and then, or maybe even throughout their entire career that affected their well-being. For some of these musicians, getting "high" seemingly provided temporary relief from these feelings. Honestly, I have never felt the need to indulge or succumb to such habits, but who knows ... I might have been judged as such! As I vividly recall, once whilst rehearsing on stage, there was a man at the venue, who made a certain assumption about my smile. He approached the front of the stage and said, 'Hey ... you always look so happy up there ...what are you using?'

This man, could neither be identified as a musician or a drug dealer, but I knew what he was getting at, and I was about to disappoint him. Contrary to his thoughts, I was not part of that crowd, and it was my intention to make sure he was aware of that fact. He looked a bit taken aback when I leant forward and without a quiver in my voice, responded, 'I am not using nothing! If I had to use drugs to play music, I would definitely stop playing the drums!'

I do not recall this man ever approaching me again, but who was to say that he would not have tried, had I not firmly put a stop to the assumption he attributed to musicians, who just happen to be visibly enjoying the flow.

Chapter 25: Home Coming & the Trio Band

Regardless of which band, musician, or performer I was supporting at gigs in the USA, from time to time, I would find a replacement drummer and ensured that I came home to my family in Bermuda. Especially at certain times of the year like Christmas, when I valued the special time spent with my family even more. This break from performing in the States, gave me time to catch up with acquaintances and close friends, like Lance Hayward, who also liked to returned to Bermuda during the festive season, and at other times.

Before Lance Hayward died, sometimes we flew home to Bermuda, to perform and support each other in annual, cultural events. One example is our participation in the Bermuda Festival, held in 1985. As reported, Lance was the first Bermudian musician to perform at the Bermuda Festival, because in previous years, invitations were limited to foreign musicians. We had flown to Bermuda that year, with three highly, regarded band musicians from New York - tenor saxophonist, Percy France, trombonist Wayne Andre and bass guitarist Major Holly. These musicians were very excited to participate in the festival, with arrangements to perform over three consecutive dates at Southampton Princess. Meanwhile, in preparation, I spent time rehearsing for Lance's performance, and then had the pleasure of supporting him, amid the lively support, of jazz enthusiasts.

Whenever we performed in Bermuda, Lance and I would have a great time reliving the old days, as well as revelling in the fact that we were once again performing on home ground, and I must admit it really felt good to be home, even if it was only for a short time. Despite having the opportunity to spend quality time with my family, and to perform locally during these visits, it was not to my advantage to stay away from my work in the USA for long periods. The ever-looming threat of being replaced by other skilled drummers, and the fear of losing touch with the US music scene was a real concern, especially for a committed musician like me. So, because of this, when my vacation or performance period ended, I knew where I had to be, and that place was the USA!

I had spent thirty years (1979 – 2009), living and working in the USA, before the pleas of my wife and daughter, who felt they had to take some action, led to my return to Bermuda. Stella and Donna had visited me in Queens, New York, to stress the importance of returning home, because as far as they were concerned, thirty years was a long time to be living away from my family. I had been there long enough, and although my frequent visits were appreciated, putting it simply, it was now time to come home!

At the time, my reputation as a skilled drummer in the USA, was almost widespread, and I was literally constantly in demand. Yet considering my wife and daughter's requests, along with my thoughts on the importance of family, I made a conscious decision to give it all up and return home. I had lived in the States where my dreams had become a reality, and having accomplished that, there should be no looking back, or so I believed! Life however, is not always that simple. In hindsight, I felt that if I had to do this all over again, I would have migrated to America before I got married, which probably meant that perhaps a part of me, would have enjoyed spending a few more years, benefiting from my performances in the US jazz world.

Returning to Bermuda, I joined the Doc Simons Trio band, with Doc Simons (Edwin Darnel Simons) and Cyril Richardson. Keyboard player Cyril Richardson (aka "The Maestro"), had performed in the USA, parts of Europe, the Inverurie and Elbow Beach Hotel. Cyril had prior recognition as a brilliant sax player, who could play across genres, from gospel to the classics. He began playing the keyboard, after recovery from an unfortunate accident, and had accepted Doc's offer to be a part of the band, when he knew for sure that I was going to be a member. Doc Simons started out as a skilled mechanic, and having practiced with Ghandi Burgess, the source of his inspiration, he became a skilled saxophonist. He was also a self-taught pianist and previous member of the Arpeggios band that supported foreign artists at the Rosebank Theatre.

I joined Doc Simons' band after he had miraculously recovered from a long period of illness, due to his resilience and fight for survival. Cyril and I had frequently encouraged Doc to slow down afterwards, but his response was always the same, 'I just can't slow down man … I have to keep moving!'

Our band played a mixture of genre for two seasons, at both Swizzle Inns on the

Island. These venues were a regular for tourists seeking to dine, whilst enjoying the music, and sampling the liquor associated with the brand name "Swizzle" (the Bermuda Rum Swizzle). The tourists attending our gigs, were always merry, (probably due to the rum!), and would show genuine appreciation and enjoyment for our performance.

At one of our gigs in July 2009 (the Jazz Veterans Concert at the Sea Breeze Terrace), Dale Butler commented favourably on our accumulated years of experience using the complimentary phrase, "Living legends" who are "still going strong" despite our age. The Bermuda Sun's news article on the event, pictured us with that said phrase "Still Going Strong" and that was true until the time Cyril and Doc sadly passed away.

Cyril Richardson, Doc Simons and Tootsie Bean (Photo courtesy of Dale Butler)

Chapter 26: Freelancing - Europe & the Far East

Three years after leaving the USA and readjusting to life in Bermuda with my family, I received some devastating news about my sister Ermine's death. She had died on the 31st October 2012, and this was such a great loss to me, particularly because we were very close. In the past, I had always confided in her about my life as a musician amongst other things, and it was hard realising and accepting the fact that she would no longer be around to extend her listening ear. It took quite a while to grieve and get over her death, but the support received from family members, and my musical engagements helped me to come to terms with the situation.

The possibility of freelancing in Europe was something that I was yearning to do, because of the simple fact that Europeans had a reputation for loving jazz music. Having travelled to Europe with Ruth Brown and Irene Reid, I knew what it was like to perform to a European audience, whose spontaneous response to a performance, would make any musician (especially one like me) feel thrilled.

The time I spent freelancing in Italy with jazz musician Paul Brown, nicknamed "PB", was a unique experience. There were two established jazz musicians by the name of Paul Brown in the USA, so I want to emphasise here that the Paul Brown I am referring to, was a black, upright bass and trumpet player and percussion teacher. Paul had founded, both the "Monday Night Jazz Series" in Connecticut and the "Greater Hartford Festival of Jazz. This was the longest running free jazz festival in the USA, with star attractions such as Herbie Hancock. Paul was also a substitute for the Count Basie and Duke Ellington bands, and had worked with greats like Fats Domino and The Drifters.

Before we departed on tour, Paul Brown's responsibility was to liaise with promoters, to sort out the freelancing contracts for Germany, Italy and Korea, including all the necessary travel and hotel arrangements. Between 2008 and 2009, Paul had established a contract with an agent, in Japan, who invited him there to perform with a band, and so Japan became part of our touring agenda. Apart from Paul Brown and me, the band members were pianist/tap dancer Danny Mixon, and a black, Japanese female vocalist from New Orleans, who had recorded with Paul previously. Most of Paul's contracted tours included one or more live recordings, and this was the case when I toured with him.

◄►

Recalling everything I had experienced freelancing with Paul Brown is not that easy at this stage, but one of the things that stood out in my mind, concerning the Italian tour, was our brief encounter with the mafia-controlled areas. I had toured Italy before, but touring the country with Paul was the first time I encountered anything to do with the Italian mafia or any mafia in question. In Italy, we had a designated chauffeur, tasked with driving us to our scheduled performances or, wherever we had to go. The problem with this was that in some areas, our chauffeur only had permission to take us so far along the route. This was for the simple fact that travelling through certain mafia-controlled areas would be restricted, unless we had an appointed mafia travel guide.

According to the way things were planned, our chauffeur was only allowed to drive us to a certain point of our destination, where an Italian mafia chauffeur, would meet and transport us through to the next stage of our journey. Understandably, Paul and I had some reservation about this type of arrangement, because hearing the word "Mafia", it was impossible to block out all the stereotypical images that were going through our minds. Yet, despite our reservations, whilst in transit to our various destinations, we all agreed on the fact that the chauffeur was cordial and friendly throughout - even if that is how it appeared on the surface. We never met the mafia boss on our travels, nor encountered any threats, but there was always a niggling thought in my mind, that made me wonder, what if, we were to step out of line!

◄►

Italy was a great place to tour with new ways to adopt. Within a short space of time, my drinking habits had changed, because most venues and restaurants very rarely offered water for refreshments. What they did offer in abundance was wine! With hardly any water on offer, I drank a lot more wine than normal. There was wine at breakfast, wine at lunch, wine at dinner and in between, so I guess I had adhered to the well-known saying, "When in Rome you do as the Romans do!"

Surprisingly drinking wine in such large quantities seemed to have very little impact on our performance. We would get on stage, expecting to feel lightheaded from the effects of the wine, only to find that nothing out of the ordinary had changed in terms of our reactions and ability to perform. I have no explanation for why this was the case; all I knew for sure, was that this wine-drinking habit had to go! It was not something I intended to continue, back home in Bermuda.

When we arrived in Berlin, one of the first places I had planned to visit was the Berlin Wall erected so many years ago. I wanted to see, with my very own eyes, this famous concrete barrier, dividing West Berlin from East Berlin, as it really was, but disappointedly, I never got the chance, even though the joys of our freelance touring continued throughout Germany. The problem was with the tour organisers. They made it virtually impossible for us band members to receive advanced, time off notification, to plan and make travel arrangements for the places we wished to visit. What I specifically liked about the Germans, was the way they enjoyed themselves and showed their love for jazz at all our shows. Due to Paul Brown's excellent advanced, promotion strategy, tickets for the shows were entirely sold out, which meant that our pre-booked venues were always packed with jazz lovers, seeking an enjoyable nightout.

In Tokyo, we were thankful at first to have an appointed chauffeur with no mafia related issues. Under normal circumstances, there was usually no need to question a chauffeur's knowledge of the local vicinity, but this chauffeur was different. After a few incidents, we began to doubt whether he really knew the locality enough to transport us to our destinations. One night on our way to a venue, we were relaxing in the back of the car when it suddenly dawned on us that we were travelling in the wrong direction. The chauffeur kept going around in circles, trying to find the right road or exit, and the reality that time was slipping by had us on the verge of panicking. If he did not get on the right route soon, we would be seriously late for our performance.

The tour manager was seated in the car, and I could see his frustration building up, when our chauffeur had difficulty turning the car around, because of the traffic. Before we knew it, he pushed opened the door, jumped out of the car, and attempted to forcefully stop the flow of traffic to allow this to happen. To us, this action was necessary, but the effect it had on the flow of traffic, was in no simple terms chaotic. Drivers tooted their horns repeatedly, as our chauffeur tried to turn the car around. Seated in the back, we could only imagine the unpleasant things they were mouthing to him in their language to vent their frustrations. Luckily for us, we arrived at the venue with enough time ahead of us, to organise ourselves for the show, which was nothing short of a miracle.

Getting around Tokyo on public transport was easier than we first thought. Because of the problems commuting by car, whenever possible, we travelled via the "Bullet Train" that arrived on the scene in 1964 - just on time for the first Tokyo Olympics. This train was shaped like a bullet, and as we had always joked, it travelled at high speed, just like a bullet, so passengers like us could expect to enjoy a bullet-speed trip to their destination.

Japanese people generally appeared to be very creative in one way or another, and they expressed admiration for those who appeared to be the same. Having toured Japan before with Ruth and Irene, I had some familiarity and respect for its associated culture, but when it came to the cuisine, this was always a problem. Eating raw foods like sushi, as opposed to cooked food, was something I simply could not stomach, without feeling ill, or ready to puke. Sports however, was a different matter. What really grabbed my attention were the Sumo Wrestling competitions. To me, those big, strong men, wrestling with hardly a stitch for covering, looked equally entertaining and peculiar all at the same time. How those scanty loincloths or Mawashi covering remained intact during a wrestling match was really a puzzle to me.

During our tour, we had performed in many Japanese venues without any problems from management or the audience. In fact, we felt welcomed and received praise for our performance wherever we performed in the country. What I found surprising was hearing some of the Japanese jazz fans, singing the lyrics to the songs we played, fluently in English. This gave the impression that they could speak English, until we tried to engage them in conversation, and realised they were very similar to us. We could not speak a word of Japanese, and they could not speak a word of English, or so it appeared. I had wondered, if this was a tactic some Japanese employed to limit conversations with foreigners, but as you may have guessed, my thoughts were never confirmed.

The Korean tours were similar to that of Tokyo, with the added benefit of cheaper prices for goods, which I took advantage of during my time there. The only issue we encountered, was associated with the division between the southern and northern areas of the country that consequently limited our performances to North Korean venues.

As we had no interest in the political climate, we choose not to view this issue as problemaltic. Our chosen venues were packed with excited jazz lovers, and we were just happy to go along with the political trend, and perform according to schedule.

The Koreans had enjoyed our performances so much, they asked us to extend our tour for an additional week. Furthermore, before we left the country, we had provisional arrangements to return to North Korea to perform at a later date, but for some unknown reason, this was never officially confirmed.

Tootsie Bean with band musicians and tour organisers in Japan.

Musician Paul Brown

Chapter 27: Awards & Events

I had received several unexpected awards during my career that were really appreciated, especially because of the special relationship I had with my drums over the years. Performing to an audience provided immense enjoyment, regardless of the location, or with whom. Apart from the satisfaction derived from this and gaining the means to make a living, I sought nothing in return. I did this for the love of the music, rather than to receive something at the end, and overall was just happy to have had the ability to make a valued contribution to the world of music.

The first of these awards, took place in November 2001, after receiving an unexpected invitation to attend an Awards Ceremony, at the Bermuda National Gallery, in Hamilton City Hall. Here, I felt honoured to receive a *"Lifetime Achievement Award",* for my longstanding work in music, presented by the Chairman of the Bermuda Arts Council. Artist Georgine R. Hill (MBE) had also received a similar award for her achievements at this event.

Later, in 2008, following in the footsteps of Ghandi Burgess and Lance Hayward, I was inducted in the Bermuda Music Hall of Fame at Shine Hayward's Music Studio. This was in recognition of my musical career spanning over a period of sixty years at that time, and the steps taken as a musician, to venture out into new pastures. Dale Butler, (Executive Director of the Atlantic Publishing House), conducted the ceremony, in addition my daughter Donna, had the task of delivering the honouring speech. Amongst the honoured inductees, were accomplished pianist, the late Maude Fox, drummer Kenneth Smith and pianist Earl Darrel. To be honest, my induction into the Hall of Fame was beyond my expectations, but I was delighted nonetheless, to receive the recognition, and for the simple fact that the organisers deemed me worthy for selection.

In the following years I received two other awards to my honour in Bermuda; *The Special Recognitions Award* in November 2013, at Hamilton City Hall, for my outstanding music contributions, overseas and in Bermuda; and *The Ambassador Award* for my commitment to music, presented at the Heard Chapel AME Church, Men's Day in 2016, by Reverend Terry Hassell.

Those Awards I remembered receiving in the USA, were from entertainers such as, saxophonist, Harold Ousley, who chose to express his appreciation for my support. I had committed myself to playing the drums for Harold's entertainment shows, organised for the children he tutored in Performing Arts, and was surprised when he showed his appreciation for my assistance, through the presentation of an Award.

Tap dancer Peg Leg Bates was another entertainer, who showed his appreciation for my support through an Award that I was delighted to receive. Mr Bates was nicknamed "Peg leg", because he had a stump in place for the leg he lost. I had no knowledge of the circumstances that led to the loss of his limb. All I knew was that despite his disability, he had amazing tap-dancing skills (comparable to any expert in the field) that he used to entertain an audience at the Apollo and other venues. After his death, his statue was erected in his home town, to honour his memory and achievements.

The invitation to perform at the 1996 Jazz Jamathon in Kingston, Jamaica, where organisers intended to honour me for my life-long contribution to music, came as another surprise. Other targeted Honourees, were pianist Barry Harris from Detroit and Lance Hayward, before the organisers learnt of his death. It was hard to believe that we were remembered after so many years had lapsed, since our last show in the country. What was also difficult to ignore, was the fact that my presence there, coupled with the respect and appreciation shown during my performance, were both reminiscent of past times. My only regret was that Lance was not there to participate, and accept his share of the honour bestowed on us, at this special event.

There were a few fund-raising events taking place in Bermuda, where featured musicians would sometimes receive an Award as part of the package. Dale Butler from Atlantic Publishing House and MyThyme Productions, for example had organised the October 2011 "Legends on the Rock" fund-raiser concert at the Leopards Club, to honour Bermuda's legendary musicians. I was amongst the featured star attractions, in addition to saxophonist Wendell (Shine) Hayward, percussionist Keith Casey and guitarist Tiny Burgess. The list also included Earl Darrell, Max Maybury, Eugene Joell and Dennis Fox. A year later at the January 2012 Cool Jade Giant Steps Concert at Pembroke Community Club, organised yet again by both Dale Butler and Darlene

Hartley, I was proud to receive recognition and an award for seventy years of service, in the entertainment world.

In addition to the Calypso Trio band, I had purposely organised a temporary Quartet to perform at specific events that reporters conveniently labelled the "Clarence Tootsie Bean Quartet". Pianist Dennis Fox, bass guitarist Tiny Burgess, saxophonist, Max Maybury and upright bass player, Clarence Burrows formed the Quartet, which was one of the star attractions at the *Keeper of the Flame Concert*, held at Pembroke Community Club.

This fund-raising initiative was intended for the creation of the new "Giant Steps Band", set to represent Bermuda, in the 2013 Cuban (Havana) International Jazz Festival. The great line-up of performers attracted a large audience, and as confirmed by news reports, in the end, they were not at all disappointed with the performances.

Tootsie Bean, Keith Caisey, vocalist Sheila Smith, keyboard player Dennis Fox, saxophonist Jade Minors & bass guitarist Stan Gilbert. (Photo courtesy of Dale Butler).

Summing Up!
(Cee Bennett-Rogers & Tootsie Bean)

Sifting through the folders of information on Mr Bean's career and listening to his narrations, it is clear to see the continuation of his passion, from youth to senior years, as he relentlessly pursued his dreams. Most of his musical experiences and performances, extended over decades, which to some extent, made it difficult to narrate in its entirety.

I came to regard Mr Bean very highly, to the extent that to simply, address this gentle, talented musician as just "Tootsie", seemed like a mark of disrespect. Therefore, during our meetings, the only appropriate title deemed worthy to show my respect, had to be, "Mr Bean".

At our first meeting, Mr Bean sat on his sofa with his wife Stella, looking somewhat pensive and subdued. I could sense that perhaps he felt obliged to do a task, for which he had some doubts, and specifically remembered him saying, 'Well … I don't know if I really want to do this. Most of my performances happened so long ago, and I'm not sure if I can recall all the details for the writing of a book!'

Mr Bean repeated this expressed sentiment on our second meeting, but knowing that his daughter, desperately wanted her beloved father's achievements captured in a book, I persevered. Mr Bean's family had collected and stored years of reported news articles and photographs about his musical career in Bermuda, USA and other places, which helped to kick-start the process. The focus on the stages of Mr Bean's career as it occurred, and his narrations, prompted by questions asked, brought back memories. In the recesses of his mind, some scenes were always there waiting to be expressed, so when the opportunity arose, he voiced them eloquently, with a passion.

Some scenes were stored in time, until I happened to ask a particular question, or required clarification and expansion of something said earlier. This served to unlock the gates of his stored experiences, and those wonderful memories came flooding back. At these times, Mr Bean was sure to say (with an endearing smile of course), 'Ahh! Now that you have asked the question, it's all coming back to me now!'

Other memories were hard to recall. They held fast, refusing to surface, and Mr Bean just had to let go. Relaying his story to the extent that he did, as I noticed, brought treasured memories of days on stage, to the forefront of his mind, and with it, a smile to his lips that caused his eyes to twinkle and his suppressed humour to surface.

When asked how he wanted to conclude his book, his first thoughts were about the youngsters that he felt needed encouragement. 'For the youngsters who might choose to read this book,' he said, 'I hope that my story will help them in any way that it can. I have tutored many students in my time and most have turned out good, so I hope that this book will provide the inspiration these young people need, to continue doing whatever good thing, they have chosen to do in life.'

He went on to add that, 'for those who have found this book inspiring in anyway, I would like you to be mindful of the fact that you should never say you can't, because all things are possible. I will also pass on the lesson learnt in life that I have always imparted to my children; nothing comes easy or will ever be handed to you; you will have to work hard for everything that you get!'

Tootsie Bean on the drums at Shine's House of Music & Entertainment.

Photos courtesy of Dale Butler

Tootsie Bean with Max Maybury (Photos courtesy of Dale Butler)

Tap Dancer Peg Leg Bates.

Photo Courtesy of Dale Butler

Tootsie Bean and Max Maybury

Tootsie Bean with Dennis Fox and Max Maybury (Photos Courtesy of Dale Butler)

Tootsie Bean entertaining in Victoria Park - (Photo courtesy of Winston O. Rogers)

(Photo's courtesy of Dale Butler)

Clarence Adolphus (Tootsie) Bean

(Photo courtesy of Dale Butler)

Tribute from son and fellow musician Mr Shelton Bean

Growing up in Bermuda, there was always music in our home. My father loved playing the drums, and because of his influence, I too became interested in learning to play this instrument to become a skilled, professional drummer. I learned to play the piano for a few years, but the drum was always the instrument that fired my interested.

When my sisters and I were young and my father was working nights, during the summer he used to take us all out, and he always behaved and treated us like a real family man. Realising that I had an interest in playing the drums, he referred me to the drummers working at the hotel, for lessons. To follow on from these introductory drumming lessons, I attended my father's drumming classes, where he tutored me before I went off to study Music. I graduated from Berklee College of Music, shortly after he left to pursue his music interests in the USA, and since then have continued to use my skills to further my career as a drummer.

My father is a great drummer, and one whose talents I have deeply respected. I admit that my style of drumming is more current, whilst my father's style is predominantly jazz, but he has broadened his skills as a result of playing the drums to different genre of music, many times in the past.

We have both acknowledged our individual talent, skills, and style of drumming, and have supported and learnt from each other over the years.

I have always had a lot of love and respect for my father. I am proud of the fact that he had set his mind to do what he wanted to do, and evidently made it happen, through hard work and sheer determination, whilst managing to do what was required as a good father, and in turn, he became my inspiration.

Drummer and music teacher Shelton Bean

Tribute from Daughter Donna Bean Raynor

I have always looked up to my dad and have always been so proud whenever he is on the drums playing. To me he is the best drummer in the world. I always tell people that my dad does not play drums but he caresses them. Such beautiful melodic sounds he made even when he was playing the Gombey beat.

My relationship with my dad has been outside the realm of music but more his support of my athletic career. Being an athlete, the support of your parents is very important during your good and bad results. Whenever I competed in a competition at the National Sports Centre, my dad had a favourite spot where he always stood and before I started any race, I looked up at that spot and there he was. I competed in a track meet a few times in New York when he was living there and he was always there to support me at the competition.

<u>One of my favourite memories that will always stand out in my mind about my dad and I:</u>

I had to go for my runs early in the mornings and my dad would always accompany me. One morning he had come in very late from work, I went to call him and my mom said he had just come home. My dad still got up and ran with me but I could see he was struggling and I told him that he did not have to run with me anymore in the mornings especially when he had late nights. He still made sure I got my runs in and still sometimes ran with me. We always had a little rivalry with who had the most trophies between his golf and my track. Of course, I won!

There were some words of wisdom that my dad gave me when I was young, and I live by those words to this day and have passed them on to my son: "Nothing will ever be handed to you, remember you have to work hard for everything that you get". Anything that I do I put in a hundred percent, and are committed to it and am passionate about it.

He lived his dream travelling overseas to live and play drums and took a chance when he decided to do it but he made it happen and I am living my life the same way by taking chances and living my best life. He always made sure we were taken care of; no matter where he was.

Thanks, Dad, for being there for me every step of the way, through my good times and bad. I always knew I could turn to you for support. I love you like life.

Tribute from Daughter Deborah Bean

I have always been so proud that my dad is the best drummer in the world. We always knew from his style of drumming that when a tune comes on the radio, it's him and we say to everyone who is within earshot 'that's my daddy'. He has an intimate relationship with his drums.

My dad supported me when I played the piano, attending my concerts and cheering me on. He was really proud when I won the TV music competition. My only regret is that I never took drum lessons. My Aunt Erm (his older sister – now deceased) later told me that my dad wanted me to be one of the first lady drummers (smile).

My favourite memory is when we were younger. On Saturday mornings when daddy had his drum students, we would go with him to the homestead on North Street and wait until he finished teaching, then afterwards we would all go to the movies. We had fun times at the homestead.

Daddy supported us all in that we did and we thank him for being there through all our ups and downs, and supporting us during our good and not so good life decisions.

He finally fulfilled his dream of living and performing overseas meeting many international stars, travelling all over the world, and making it to Carnegie Hall.

Thank you, daddy, for being you and supporting us in all that we did.

Daddy I love you like life!

Tribute from Daughter Jeannette Trott

Dad this is for you,

I know from our talks you used to worry about your adult children not getting along. Daddy, we are all right now. I have love for all of them.

Dad August 14th 2019 was your 89th birthday, and you said , "I am staying at 88", I thought that was so funny but daddy you have many more birthdays to come.

Dad I miss our lunch dates on Mondays at the Spot Restaurant and on Wednesdays if we could not do Mondays, also I miss the few bus rides we were able to fit in.

Dad I cherish all the time that we have spent together it means the world to me, one thing that I always look forward to was our talks on the phone. I love you with all my heart.

Jeannette

Tribute from Mr John Woolridge
(MA Edu Music, Pianist, Producer, Composer & Educator)

The "Chewstick Foundation" had contacted me to perform a tribute song to Lance Hayward. They had asked if I could have veteran Tootsie Bean perform with me. I was excited about a chance to play with someone who was a noted legend among local Bermuda musicians.

It is important to note that Bermuda was a major performance hub for "A List" entertainers from around the world in the 1940 – 1970 and Tootsie was known among the mainstream of the music industry.

So, Tootsie sat down to the drums and my high school drum set came alive! Without verbal communication, we began to interact and answer phrases using our instruments. We grinned and laughed as we had gone through the song with confidence and ease.

So, on the night of the concert, I was privileged to witness the mark of a great Artist.
There is an internal gear that is activated in the master musician-performer. When I counted off the tune, Tootsie gave an unrehearsed drum fill and off we went into that "next gear"

Tootsie drove the groove, a pulsating drive on the ride cymbal and snapped out accents on the snare. Whency, my brother; an amazing bassist, walked in phrase playing with strong colours. He added answer accents to Tootsie.

Tootsie started to grin as I aggressively punched out chords and lines. We teasingly explored the melodies and rhythms, which mounted in intensity until the solos.

Tootsie was on fire he was flamboyant, facile, and articulate in his solo, and as concluded the audience gave a rousing applause. We played the head and finished, and the crowd immediately stood to give us a standing ovation.

I felt so blessed to have had the opportunity to share the bandstand with this music legend.

Tribute from Saxophonist Mr Wendell ("Shine") Hayward (BA Professional Music)

Having grown up in the church had me isolated somewhat from the senior, main stream, local musicians. Most I knew only by name. It was not until my late teens that I actually managed to see some of them perform. These would be Ghandi Burgess, Lance Hayward, Hubert Smith, The Talbot Brothers, Ernie Leader and of course Clarence "Tootsie" Bean (to name a few).

Lance and "Tootsie" were the first that I became aware of, who found it better to travel overseas to take their musical talents to the next level. Whilst the two of them performed often together, Lance held on to a solo gig in the Village for many years (until his death), whilst "Tootsie (Uncle Toot) performed and recorded with many other international artists, the most popular of these being Irene Reid.

Apparently, Uncle Toot was well sought after in New York, and was no stranger around the heaviest of hitters. Uncle Toot would come home and grace us with his presence for only short periods, but one could always see the admiration, love and respect that he generated amongst all of the local musicians. His performance was always similar to a workshop for local drummers. You could see the gleam in their eyes, as they would inch closer to the stage to take note of all of his licks. His feel and timing were impeccable. His solos always brought a level of excitement, as he never forgot his roots and would find a place in his solo to introduce the whistle, accompanied by the sound of the Gombey rhythm.

Uncle Toot started to lose a bit of his hearing and was convinced to return home to spend time with his family. This gave me an opportunity to really get to know him. Uncle Toot would invite me to perform at his church, which he attends and plays the drums every Sunday He frequented my club as a performer and observer, and had his birthday celebration at the club. I had the opportunity to actually work with him at the Swizzle Inn after the passing of "Doc" (his sax player), and then I honoured him as Bermuda's Last Living Legend at one of my International Jazz Day Celebrations.

One of the nicest, easy going, down to earth, humble, gifted and talented musicians/gentleman anyone would want to meet, I am happy to call Clarence "Tootsie" Bean (Uncle Toot) My Friend.

Tootsie Bean at home with his drums. 2018. Photo by Winston O. Rogers

Photo courtesy of Dale Butler

Made in the USA
Coppell, TX
21 April 2021

54283272R00081